MW00720527

FAMILY MATTERS

FAMILY MATTERS

JUDITH TIMSON

HarperCollins*Publishers*Ltd

FAMILY MATTERS

Copyright © 1996 by Judith Timson

All rights reserved. No part of this book may be used or reproduced in any manner whatsoever without prior written permission except in the case of brief quotations embodied in reviews.
For information address HarperCollins Publishers Ltd, Suite 2900, Hazelton Lanes, 55 Avenue Road, Toronto, Canada M5R 3L2.

http://www.harpercollins.com

The following essays are original to this publication: "Snapshots," "Crossing Over," "Selected States of Modern Living," "The Mother of All Projects," "Girlfriends," "Savages," "Building a Better Boy," "Emily Will Be Thirteen in the Year 2000," and "Gay Pride and Mockingbirds." "Diana's Revenge" and "Babes, Bitches, Bimbos and Other True Lies" appeared, in similar form, in *Maclean's*. All other essays have appeared, in similar form, in *Chatelaine*.

First Edition

Canadian Cataloguing in Publication Data

Timson, Judith
Family matters

Collection of essays from Chatelaine and new material.
ISBN 0-00-638057-3

1. Family - Humor. I. Title.

PS8589.I552F3 1996   C818'.5402   C95-933311-8
PR9199.3.T55F3 1996

96 97 98 99 ❖ HC 10 9 8 7 6 5 4 3 2 1

Printed and bound in the United States

For Martin, Jonathan and Emily

CONTENTS

ACKNOWLEDGMENTS

*I*t's been almost five years since Mildred Istona, the former editor of *Chatelaine*, invited me to write a personal column on family life. I thank her for starting me on this voyage. Rona Maynard, the current editor, has continued to offer me a prominent place in *Chatelaine*, as well as excellent editorial advice and support. I thank the magazine's wonderful staff for their help and forbearance over the years. Carolyn Lim Chua, *Chatelaine's* editorial and administrative manager, has always been helpful, especially in compiling the original list of articles that appear in this book.

Iris Tupholme, publisher/editor-in-chief of HarperCollins Publishers Ltd, has my gratitude for her enthusiasm, insights and sharp-eyed editing. As do Jem Bates for his deft copy-editing, Jocelyn Laurence for her proofreading extraordinaire, and Nicole Langlois for her last minute shepherding of the manuscript into print. I'd also like to thank Suzanne DePoe, my agent, who embarked on her own adventure as a new mother as I was finishing this book.

A small group of talented and generous friends gave me sound writing advice: Linda Hossie, Marni Jackson, Ann Dowsett Johnston, Margaret McConaghay, and Jane O'Hara. I also thank them—and a larger group of equally wonderful friends—for picking me up, dusting me off, and urging me on more times than I can mention. This group includes Alison Heppner, Susan Goldberg, Vicky Stott, Diana McVean, and Mary-Ellen Mattice, but there are many more women, men, and children whose wisdom, insights, and revelations about the way we live our lives today inform this book. I'd also like to thank Fern Small and Elizabeth Qualben for helping me, in very different ways, to make important decisions about the book.

Author Philip Roth once quoted a Czech poet as saying, "If a writer is born into a family, that family is finished." My sympathies and thanks go to the members of my own family—my brother Jeff, his wife Cherie, and their children, my father Ray Timson and his family, and most of all, to my mother Emily Timson who, with her warmth and humanity, is my most treasured ally. As for my husband's remarkable family—his parents Dodo and Lyone, his siblings, Erik and Alison, Sara and Danny, and Maxine—and all my nieces, nephews and other relatives on both sides of our families who have good-naturedly played important roles in this book: I feel lucky to know them all. I also offer a special thank you to Nanny—Frances Finestone—no longer with us, but very present in this book.

It's obvious, however, that I owe everything, from the first to the last word, to my husband Martin, and to our children Jonathan and Emily. They have been as wonderful as any family could be, about the writing, about this crazy, lovely life we've fashioned together. Remarkably, all three of them, but especially Martin, have, with unfailing grace, put up with being characters in a column, perhaps because they know the truth: *this can't go on forever*. I love them, and thank them, with all my heart.

FAMILY MATTERS

SNAPSHOTS

I arrived home from work several years ago, from the office I used to rent when the kids were younger. I was tired, hungry, and really looking forward to seeing my children. My husband was working late. I came in the back door, and instead of cries of delight, I was greeted by two impossibly grumpy kids. (My theory is, often they don't know they're mad at you for leaving until you walk back in.) Our part-time baby-sitter said goodbye and assured me she had already fed them, so I knew it couldn't be hunger that was turning them into monsters.

After struggling to get my coat off, while holding my daughter in my arms and listening to my son, I made a Lean Cuisine—one of those instant chicken and rice delights. As I began eating, both kids continued to rage at me in imperious voices: *Mommy I want, Mommy I need, Mommy you said I could.* . . . I sat there for a few minutes, and then, overwhelmed, I bolted upstairs, taking my plate with me. I ran into the bathroom, locked the door, sat down on the toilet, and in between sobs, ate my crummy little boiled-in-the-bag dinner, wondering, what's wrong with this picture? Have we come this far from "Leave it to Beaver" land? You call this a family life?

The truth, I now know, is that nothing was wrong with that picture that a little humour and perspective couldn't fix. No, that scene was merely a snapshot from modern life—Mom works, Mom comes home tired, kids rightfully erupt, Mom feels defeated, and locks self in bathroom. Does anyone have a problem with that?

Here is another snapshot. It is a spectacular day in August, and we are at a cottage we rent in northern Ontario. Our daughter Emily, now eight, is dancing on the beach, her petite body literally jumping for joy at the sun and sand and sheer luxury of it all. Jonathan, serious and handsome at ten, is in the bright yellow paddle boat, manoeuvring it around with a look of surprised competence on his face, and Martin, my husband, free for two weeks from the worries of his small investment company, is getting the canoe ready for a solo paddle on a quiet lake. He looks over at me, sitting on the sand with a book, and smiles: "*It doesn't get any better than this.*" My heart catches as I contemplate us all, within a yard or two of each other, busy and sunburnished and perfectly content in our own and each other's company. Later, there will be a monster Monopoly game that will end in tears (and a dark suspicion on my part that my husband cheated me out of Park Place) but that is another story.

Having a family has moulded me, changed me, made me open my eyes in a way that a previous decade or so of living my life as a single, childless writer never could. Author Paul Theroux has observed: "I did not understand a thing I read, nor did I begin to write well, until I married and had children. . . . the ritual and romance of adulthood bred such intense emotions in me that one day I would see myself as a victim and the next day as a hero. But I was simply being a husband and father." Or wife and mother. Such joy, such anxiety, such hope and imperfection. Such relentless routine, so many macaroni and cheese dinners—all of it set against a backdrop of contemporary stresses and challenges, and the cacophany of all those doomsayers and social analysts: the family can't survive, it is finished, kaput, the centre is not holding—except there is this beautiful day and three people who define my life are dancing in the sunlight . . .

With some trepidation, I introduce you to this family. My husband

Martin is tall, dark-haired, generous-hearted, and also, yes I swear, absent-minded and memory-challenged to a degree I have never met in a man so young. And here are our children. You can see them in these verbal snapshots—Emily, with her straight blond bangs, small face, and true grit, self-assured, animal-loving, deep at eight, with endless stories to write and pictures to draw. And her brother Jonathan—amazingly complex at ten—plays piano, keeps his distance from team sports, can carry on a conversation with anyone, loves acting and music and laughing till he drops on the floor (and also occasionally snorts root beer through his nose).

And then there is me—the I of the storm. I was hired by *Chatelaine* magazine five years ago to write a personal column about family life, and that I have done, sifting through the detritus of our lives and coming up, not with ultimate answers, but at least with some key questions: are we really a functioning family, a work in progress, a failed experiment? Yes, yes, and yes. Do lesbians have more fun? Maybe, maybe not. And why does my husband spend so much time in the bathroom? Because he wants to.

But this job does have a few occupational hazards: rampant use of the first-person pronoun, middle-of-the-night worries (have I turned my family into cartoon characters?), and some serious mud-wrestling in my mind over subject matter (I keep thinking I'll get to the heart of gender conflict and then for some reason I find myself writing about trolls . . . though maybe that is getting to the heart of it).

There is, as well, a much more central issue that daunts anyone who wants an audience today in this, the age of cultural diversity and terrifying economic realities: how do you justify your own experiences as relevant? All I can do is offer you the truth of my life—there are days when I ace it (I personally counted, oh, twelve last year), there are days when I'd like to have a live-in (or perhaps merely a drive-by) family therapist to help me deal with the collapsing child-care arrangements, the needy children, the dwindling bank account and precarious professional life, the gnawing sense of failure and doom on one or more fronts. And then there are the days in between, which I guess are just called life.

I believe we have the potential to create satisfying lives for ourselves and our families, lives that succeed on all these difficult levels. Family life today is a struggle, and you are not crazy if you think it is the hardest thing you've ever done. There isn't a woman alive who, down in the basement and slinging laundry into the machine at 11 PM, hasn't said to herself: "This isn't quite what I meant." It is then that American author Naomi Wolf's observation that "we have gone further than our mothers, further than our grandmothers, we have gone further than anyone ever told us it was safe to go" can take on a whole new meaning.

I spend a great part of my day talking to other women—my friends, my colleagues, my readers—who tell me about their daily lives and how, at that particular moment, whatever they have cobbled together works or doesn't work. I tell you this: *every day*, one of them tells me something that makes my jaw drop. I see them every morning, hustling to the subway, having dropped off the children; I see them during the day, determinedly wheeling strollers into local coffee shops; and in the evening, I meet them as we're picking up our kids from school or daycare. And I'm always struck again by the complexity of their—our—lives, and the ingenuity of most women in coming up with solutions. It is the daily heroism of their lives that touches me. I believe that women today have a hunger for information and affirmation about the real lives they are living, both inner and outer.

These columns, however much they were laboured over, are still just snapshots—of an issue, a feeling, a phase—in my own life. I often wrote out of the need to understand something happening in our home life. I would write about, say, a bad morning we experienced, and then, of course, we wouldn't have another one for weeks. Meanwhile, a letter would arrive from an impatient reader telling me to snap out of it and, furthermore, get my kids to make their own lunches.

Some of these columns were written when my children were much younger than they are today. But I don't want to change the age-specific references. They span nearly five years of family life, so they should and do embrace everything from pre-school tantrums to pre-teen sexual awareness. They don't, alas, deal with the baby years. (*I remember some brown couches, lots of crying, and one summer with cartons of two different-sized diapers—extra large and newborn—everywhere. That's about it. Thank God I've got the pictures to remind me of the rest.*) But they do encompass most of the possible permutations of daily life available to a mother/writer: at home with my children, part-time work in a rented office, part-time work at home, and now, with the children in school all day, full-time work from my home.

Many of these pieces offer scenarios that could only happen in the nineties—taking our children, for instance, to the gay pride parade. Others are about the more timeless aspects of family life— religion, death, and I'm sure I've got taxes in there somewhere.

I make no claim, however, that this collection, of both my columns and new writing, is an all-encompassing look at the life of a modern mom: we all know motherhood is not a quality trade paperback. It's not even a movie (although I do see it as a theme park . . . *and over here, ladies and gentlemen, get ready to ride the scariest ride of all, the hormonal roller-coaster! . . .*). No, motherhood is your guts spilled out onto the breakfast table every morning, along with the Cheerios. It never stops being that. (Maybe it will when the kids reach their forties . . .)

I have loved writing these columns, loved running what I view as the complaints department of modern family life. Only occasionally have I been startled by a reaction. I was talking to a former colleague the other day, and he said to me: "My wife and I read your column, and we say to each other, 'Well, at least we're not *that* bad.'" Which kind of takes your breath away, doesn't it?

We all think the circumstances of our domestic lives, of how we came to be a family, are unique. We repeat the stories, savour the details, pore over the photos that tell of a remarkable odyssey—we met, fell in love, married, had children. It is at once the most banal and the most exciting story ever told, even if it does, for many people today, end—or begin anew—in divorce court.

When we married, my Great Uncle Tom, a New England gentleman, wrote us a congratulatory card, saying we were about to embark on "life's greatest adventure." He is no longer alive, but I think of that line often as I stagger through my days, convinced on Mondays and Wednesdays that this life we've fashioned just isn't going to fly, and on Thursdays and Saturdays that it's holding together after all. *Life's greatest adventure* . . . it has a nice ring to it. Maybe that's what we should call the theme park.

THE TRUTH ABOUT FAMILY VALUES

*O*ne man, one woman, one young boy, and his smaller sister. If you photographed us walking arm in arm (and my hair was combed), we would be perfect material for a family-values propaganda campaign. But if you dug beneath the surface, you'd find all of us thinking slightly subversive thoughts. The train-of-thought cartoon bubble over my husband's head would probably read: "Now my life is even *more* complicated—I'm supposed to show up for every daytime event in my kids' lives, pay the mortgage, *and* be a success. Why can't I just lie down?" And the bubble over my head would read: "You think this is easy? I've got an article due next week, I'm trying to keep the house organized and the kids happy, and even though I love my husband and my children, I sometimes have this rage that won't go away." The bubble over my son's head would read "*#!!," because kids today are so rude you cannot believe it, while the bubble over my daughter's head would be "I'm going to wear what I want, do what I want, and climb a big mountain when I grow up."

Overworked, challenging traditional thinking to the point of domestic anarchy, allowing major static from our kids, today's families struggle on, fighting to keep themselves above water financially, and snatch a few minutes of joy somewhere along the line. Some of us even manage to indulge in that profoundly middle-class luxury of examining the very *idea* of family life.

Then, in came these hackneyed politicians to tell us what we really need is to return to "family values," a phrase that became an instant cliché and struck a chord in many of us. Is it possible we have all screwed up and created a world where families literally cannot flourish? I wonder about all the kids who are hungry, emotionally and physically, about the rising instances of abuse and neglect. I wonder, is this the year that teachers will tell us fiercely to stop using them as social workers? Is this the year the definitive study will show that children of divorce, or children of mothers who work, are more likely to be ax-murderers? Frankly, I think working mothers are more likely to be ax-murderers. At times, we are pushed to the wall. But then, our stay-at-home counterparts do not fare any better psychologically. The truth is, we are all pedalling as fast as we can.

There is no doubt we all have a deep unease about our complex lives today, a desire for a safer haven. But there is no safe haven, and there never was. American historian Stephanie Coontz, in her book *The Way We Never Were: American Families and the Nostalgia Trap* (published by Basic Books), concluded that there was no halcyon time for family life, that families have always had to struggle to survive economically, and to stay intact emotionally, that we need to come to terms with the fact that the family has never been perfect, has never quite worked—that is the nature of the beast.

So what is the family-values crowd harking back to? Is it the fifties, when men were imprisoned in their grey flannel straitjackets, working so much they were barely home, while women were advised by their doctors that a little antidepressant might be in order for that "blue" feeling they experienced as they watched their lives being defined by kitchen walls and the needs of others? Or is it perhaps the Victorian era they long for, when men and women led profoundly separate lives, and sexuality was a matter of confusion and shame?

And what values, exactly, do they have in mind? Is it the "respect" that kept most children from challenging their parents because they feared they would be physically punished if they did? Or the value of an intact marriage at all costs, no matter whether there was alcoholism, abuse, or profound emotional alienation? Or maybe it is the value of a woman being seen and not heard.

The irony is that in some ways, I think, we are closer to a good model of family life now than we were in the fifties, as we try to redefine family life to include such laudable ideas as gender equality, and a kinder, gentler way to bring up kids. My own husband, and the men he knows, has done more with our children in ten years than most fathers of the previous generation did in the entire span of raising their children. There is also a recognition today that family life does not take place in a vacuum—I go into the schools and I see parents (more than a hundred of them volunteered in one year in our school), some in business attire, present in the schools during the day in a way they never were when I was growing up.

Why aren't these values honoured, these values that have sprung partly from the women's movement toward more equality in the home, from more women taking their newfound assertiveness and competence into the schools? Instead, that phrase "family values" is as loaded with false sentimentality as apple pie and motherhood, and as empty of real meaning. Is there anyone out there who is *against* family values? I'll bet if you wandered into a leather bar, at least one of its denizens would grow misty-eyed over the concept.

What was and is wrong with the current family-values debate is not that it spurs us on in our worthwhile search for ways to keep families of all kinds together and help our kids function in the face of enormous stress—marriages that fail almost as much as they succeed, an economy buried in quicksand. And the problem is not that it reinforces the idea that children need as much hands-on nurturing as they can get from both parents. It is that many people use it—and the phrase "family values" itself—as a code word for exclusion. *This is what a family looks like and if you don't fit the bill—if you're gay, divorced, a single parent, a single person—too bad.*

Well, we *do* fit the bill and we are still not buying it: one woman, one man, one young girl, and her older brother. Give us our rage at times, our confusion, even our domestic anarchy. But please, don't return us to traditional family values. We will make our own, thank you.

MORNING GORY

*I*t is 7:30 AM and there is a wild woman loose in my house. She is barking out one-word commands at two little children and one grown man, all of whom are not trembling in her wake. Yes, it's me, trying to wrestle our morning into submission. Mom vs. the volcano, one of my friends calls it.

Whatever it is, I don't like it. I hear myself say, "It's garbage day—again" pointedly at my husband and I think, we'll never be immortalized as the Spencer Tracy and Katharine Hepburn of our time—but then again, Spencer probably didn't go through the five stages of grief on the issue of garbage. Right now *my* witty dialogue partner is rounding the corner from denial, experiencing a burst of anger, and will soon move into the acceptance phase, bending to empty the can under the sink with a certain weariness that tugs at my heart.

Meanwhile, our four-year-old daughter has been trying to engage us both in fashion wars since, oh, it seems like dawn, black tights vs. white tights, twirly skirt vs. leggings, black-and-white striped top vs. turtleneck, until I am reduced to a blithering heap—"Oh, wear it, wear it, just *wear* it," I moan and escape downstairs. My husband goes resolutely back upstairs to do emotional mop-up, and I—cringing in the kitchen—feel somewhat relieved to hear his voice cracking as he pleads with her to let him go to work, where presumably he is regarded as a fully functioning adult and not a man whose major role is to provide valet service for someone barely three feet tall.

From the third floor come the sounds of *Police Academy* instead of our six-year-old son whistling merrily as he dons his school clothes and heads down to the kitchen ready for another great day. I call (well, call loudly), "TIME TO GET DRESSED; TIME TO COME DOWN FOR BREAKFAST!" And of course I'm greeted with, in due course, *his* existential wardrobe crisis: "My turtleneck's not tight enough!" Is it just me being paranoid or am I the only one of my friends to have produced *two* really eccentric children?

As I darkly ponder family-therapy bills for the rest of our natural lives, I ask myself this question: do other women's children get dressed docilely in the morning and sit down for a congenial bowl of Shreddies, while the parents have time for an affectionate joke or two? And if so, why is it that my house on occasion gets swallowed up by the Morning That Ate the Nuclear Family for Breakfast?

Oh, we've had our share of those mornings when the coffee tastes great, the sun is pouring in, and the kids are sitting there being more wonderful than we ever imagined possible. When there is even a little something left over for the two of us—a glance that says more to me than "Are we out of cream cheese again?" Those mornings are so good I want to document them somehow, so that when the morning gory begins anew, I'll have some hope, some warm memories of the way we were.

Theorists of the modern family (wait—that might be me!) tell us that contemporary life, with its two-job, half-a-heart family, is to blame for a level of anxiety that corrodes even our basic morning routines. The stakes are higher as we rush around, with some parents leaving the house as early as 6 AM to drop their children off at daycare or with sitters. And women, careening from soothing caregiver to army sergeant marshalling the troops for another day in the jungle, are both the villains and the victims of the ante having been upped. Which is a nice way of saying that modern life—or is it family life?—has turned me into a bitch.

Sociology is cold comfort, though, in the face of reality. Whether or not I'm a social statistic, it's my job—and my joy—to make it work. I guess it's lucky that I find the down side more interesting than the perfection. And it's a good thing, too, that my husband and I are occasionally able to phone each other mid-morning and give each other courage for the next round. It may not be up to Spencer and Katharine's standards, but it's not half bad.

On the days I do go to my office, I look covertly at the other women scurrying along the street, knowing that many of them, too, have lived an entire life of domestic drama before the work bell sounds. I wonder if their children were balky or needy that morning. I wonder if they had a fight (or a fling) with their partners, or if they faced the morning alone and lonely. I wonder whether they were up all night nursing a sick child. And most of all, I wonder as they walk into their offices and turn to their work, how they can put it all behind them. Truthfully, I can't.

SLEEPING AROUND

*L*ast night I slept with two males again. One of them was tall, dark, and handsome, the other short, fairer-haired, and incredibly intense. I was squashed in the middle, listening, on one hand, to some full-fathom-five snoring, and on the other, to something vaguely asthmatic, a sort of wheeze with a catch in it. With these two bodies sacked out on either side of me, I lay awake wondering how my night-life had come to such a neck-wrenching pass. (Two pillows, three heads, much noise.)

Occasionally, the tall, dark, and handsome one would wake up and whisper to me, "We've got to do something about this." Once, the shorter sleeper opened his eyes and murmured something about seeing a gigantic snake, which sent me into analysis overdrive. (What, on top of everything else I have to worry about Freudian images in my son's dreams? . . . Maybe this is what healthy six-year-old boys dream about.)

Many, many hours later, it was morning. I did not know what I looked forward to least—getting through the day, or encountering whatever night-time follies were ahead.

I hate labelling everything a trend, but I have to say that this generation of parents seems to be experiencing one gigantic sleep problem. Just check out the self-help shelves in major bookstores if you doubt it. One title I gratefully glommed onto was *How to Solve Your Child's Sleep Problem*, and the suggestions in it were useful for almost a week.

The truth is, some of us—a great many of us—have trouble putting our kids to bed, or getting them to stay there all night long. I know families whose sleeping arrangements evoke Third World conditions. They all sleep in the same room, often piled up on the floor while three seriously decorated bedrooms lie empty. I know one ten-year-old girl whose parents claim she has never, *ever* slept in her own room. I met one couple who simply gave up and purchased a king-size futon and invited the family to bunk there permanently. If God had wanted us all together in one bedroom, would She have given us children's designer wallpaper?

And so the parents become night nomads, wandering from unoccupied bed to unoccupied bed as the night of the living horror progresses. Baby sister in with Mom, Dad grabs baby sister's bed, meanwhile older sister, hearing the rustle of activity, decides her room is too lonely and joins baby sister and Mom; Mom then gets restless and sneaks out to older sister's room, lights on, lights off . . . In some countries, they torture people like this.

Some women have confessed to me that if it is not their children, it is their husbands who keep them awake. Recently, both my husband and son suffered synchronized anxiety attacks at 3 AM, so I had stereo angst—one moaning about his bank balance, the other reliving a menacing encounter in the school yard.

In our house, we have an intermittent problem with one child, while the other only wanders in occasionally to give us a dream update—"First there was this bad guy, then a dalmatian got sick. . . ."

New York wit Fran Lebowitz once extolled sleep as "death without the responsibility." I have been a fan of that kind of delicious coma-like sleep ever since I went through early motherhood and realized that I would never again experience it. When I learned that sleep deprivation could possibly be a defence for murder, I understood exactly why. I have obsessed about sleep, hoarded it, valued it, lusted after it, planned my stealthy campaign to finally, *finally* achieve it with as much precision as Margaret Thatcher organized the invasion of the Falkland Islands. It did not involve drugging my children or threatening them with bodily harm, but everything else was fair game.

When I mentioned this problem to my mother, she managed to be tactfully bewildered. "Well, I just don't know what to think," she said. "Unless my memory is faulty, I don't remember you or your brother ever doing this, nor any of my friends going through it."

So, what's wrong with us? Are we loving our children too much, afraid to let them go in the night, too lazy or tired to get up and put them back where they belong? Or are we giving them the kind of comfort that we ourselves were denied as children because our parents were told by the child-rearing experts of the day that it just wasn't right? Are today's children more neurotic? Are today's parents more neurotic? Can we possibly blame this on rock videos?

Some psychologists say get your children out of your bed, others say what's the harm? One therapist I know of confessed his daughter slept with them all the time and *he* loved it. Well, loving it is not the point. We got married because, among other things, we liked sleeping together. At no point did we discuss third parties joining us.

Tonight, we will make it right. Tonight, everyone will go to her or his own bed and stay there. Tonight will be the first night of the rest of our lives.

SAFE AND SORRY

*W*hen he was seven and a half, I allowed my son to go to the corner store alone for the first time. His mission was to buy green garbage bags for us (and a treat for himself and his sister). Before he left the house, I did a quick street-proof review. Did he know about strangers? What to do if one approached him? What about parked cars, traffic, and looking both ways before he crossed the street? At last, after restlessly enduring my maternal overdrive, he set off, money clutched tightly in hand.

It was a long ten minutes. Finally he burst through the front door triumphant: "Mom," he shouted, "I made it back alive!" We are talking here of a distance of under two blocks in broad daylight, but I had somehow made those two blocks out to be as dangerous as a New York alley under a full moon. Here was an important moment in a child's life—the first time his mother told him he was big enough and wise enough to do an errand by himself—and I had imbued it with a paranoia that would not be out of place in a Martin Scorsese film: *Mean Streets Part 2—My Trip to the Variety Store.*

Embarrassed, I spent a few minutes berating myself for being neurotic, and then came to the conclusion it was not my fault. (This happens a lot when you're a parent.) I had simply been swept along by the fear that has become standard in urban life—that our children are not safe on our streets, in our shopping malls, or in any public place.

You hardly ever see very young children alone on city streets any more, even on a glorious day when they could be kicking a ball down the street, scooping up leaves, or doing nothing in particular. Instead, today's children travel through the city with parents or nannies or relatives who are as vigilant as Brink's security guards.

Today's young children live, in urban environments at least, a hothouse existence, their casual encounters with friends mutated into pencilled-in "play dates," their imaginations challenged, if not stifled, by overscheduled days that are replete with everything but freedom. I fiercely rail against this violation of childhood and the loss of open-ended free time (the loss, too, of solitude) uncontaminated by adult enthusiasms. I wonder if it is going to turn our children into fearful, dependent beings, with no tolerance at all for the normal hurly-burly of city life.

I wonder, too, at the absurd contradictions in our cultural and social lives. There are many parents who would allow their children to watch *Terminator 2*, but not to walk half a block by themselves. The former, of course, reinforces the latter. Movies and television today provide a grim reflection of what we apparently truly believe about ourselves—that there is a heart of darkness within, where violence and mayhem await vulnerable children.

But statistically, it makes no sense. Child abductions by a stranger are so rare, even in a metropolitan city the size of Toronto, that we still remember the name of each child who was abducted. Of course, the reason we remember the names is that these children were murdered, and their names became headlines. In stranger abductions, you rarely get a second chance.

That is probably why the police are so cautious in advising parents how to keep their children safe—teach them never to play alone outside, but always with friends (which makes sense); teach them that adults rarely ask a child for help; and most important of all, the rule we would like to tattoo on our children's consciousness, teach them to always let their parents know their whereabouts. In our house, it's called the "check first" rule: before you set one foot outside the yard, you check first to see that it's all right.

But attempting to be careful while also loosening the reins selectively is hard. When I called the police for advice and statistics, they faxed me a pamphlet, and right away I felt my anxiety level rising: I had completely forgotten rule number ten—what had I been thinking, to let him carry money *in his hand* to the corner store? He could have been mugged! (Well, it says so in the pamphlet.)

The police officer I spoke to enthused about a privately produced video that was, in his opinion, the latest word in street-proofing. But after I talked to the producer of the video on the phone, I wanted to barricade the house and send my children to school in an armoured van. "In the abduction sequence," the producer said in a solemn "voice-over" tone, "we don't show any bodies, but we do show the shoreline where one was found."

The video comes equipped with a parental viewing guide, and is meant to be shown in both schools and homes for a family-team approach to street-proofing. Who knows? Maybe we'll get it.

But why does it have to be like this?

REFERENCES REQUIRED

*T*he other day, I was cleaning out an old briefcase. Tucked inside, in my handwriting, was an advertisement I had considered placing in a newspaper some years ago: *Experienced, caring baby-sitter wanted for two days a week to help look after happy two-year-old and newborn. Refs required.*

It actually made my stomach jolt when I saw it. I cannot think of anything that stirs up more contradictory feelings in women than searching for someone else to care for our children. There's worry of course—how can you be sure the person you hire will actually be loving, caring, and trustworthy, that she won't be the kind of psychopath Rebecca De Mornay made famous in that evil flick *The Hand That Rocks the Cradle*, or more likely, that she won't make that one crucial mistake that leads to unspeakable events?

(Is there a woman away from her kids who has not experienced that clammy feeling that something is terribly wrong at home, that her kids are in . . . danger? Usually, they are not, although they might be watching *Geraldo* with their sitter.)

And then there is guilt. We are, after all, only a generation removed from the myth, if not the reality, of the hearth 'n' home mom. Never mind that, for me, as well as for most women, economic realities make the choice to stay home with my children a luxury. It still has to be squared away with oneself (let alone one's mother), this notion of ceding the care of your children to a woman who will almost automatically be from another culture, and who will have her own complicated story of how she came to be knocking on your door.

Of course, exposing our children to another culture should go on the plus side of the ledger, but somehow it seems to dredge up more contradictory feelings, as evidenced by one joke that was making the rounds a while back: there is an entire group of North American children who, when they are grown, will be searching for their roots in the Philippines. That joke, of course, has little to do with culture and race, and everything to do with guilt.

I don't know of a woman who has not been done wrong by a baby-sitter, from the relatively harmless situation, such as when a friend of mine noticed that her departing baby-sitter had lifted her best sweater, to the traumatic: I once witnessed, in the park, a sitter verbally abusing a child, shouting at her over and over again, until the child cowered in her stroller. Did that child's mother even know what a horror her sitter was?

Then, there are the stories the nannies warm themselves by the fire with—the mothers who expect them to do absolutely everything from balancing the family chequebook to being the emotional mainstay for their children (without, of course, being allowed to take credit for it). The quest for *the* nanny reached its nadir in an ad I saw once in a major newspaper, in which a woman shamelessly wrote: "I am looking for nothing less than a total replacement for myself." To which the only rational response is: "Why did you bother to have children in the first place?"

The truth is, there are great sitters, good-enough sitters, and lousy sitters, and there is an equal proportion of the same kinds of mothers employing them. Most mothers who employ sitters are not from the privileged enclave, they are middle-class, and pressed for money.

I never did place that ad in the newspaper about the happy two-year-old and the newborn. Through the nanny grapevine, I found

Grace, a young woman from the Philippines who stayed with us for almost three years, and whose younger sister, Zusette, took her place when she left. They were—are—both enormously competent, caring, and smart women. And while the relationship between Grace and me was frayed toward the end—she was ready for another kind of job in the wider world—Zusette and I worked, and worked hard, to have a good relationship for the three and a half years she was with us.

But oh, the balancing act! There were times I worried about her almost as much as I worried about my kids. She was young, pretty, and ambitious—she had a university degree and eventually wanted to be a lawyer—and, if she came in stony-faced, which she did on occasion, I would (sometimes seething inside, I admit) try to make an effort to find out what was wrong. Often, I got nowhere.

My children adored her. She made the most delicate, artful birthday cards for them; she was meticulous about the way they looked, their cleanliness, their manners. She introduced my daughter, as a baby, to rice—and to this day, it is, unadorned, Emily's favourite thing to eat. (I often think that when she gobbles that rice, even at the age of eight, Emily always connects it to the enormous love that Zusette offered her.)

On the other hand, we clashed over some important matters. On the subject of boys, Zusette was clearly coming from another culture. I had to gently and then firmly tell her several times that she need never tell my son that boys couldn't cry.

Once, for an article I was writing, I interviewed a woman whose job it was to act as an advocate for foreign domestic workers who often ended up in terrible situations, literally being held hostage by employers who threatened them with deportation if they didn't work punitively long days. I asked this woman what was the best advice she could give someone about to employ a nanny, and she said firmly, "Don't treat her as a member of your family. She isn't—and she knows it. Give her your respect as an employee doing a difficult and demanding job, pay her proper wages, and treat her fairly under the law."

Well, I hope I did all that, but you can't stop the heart from getting involved. When the kids were finally both in school all day and it was time for Zusette to move on, she and I began the intricate process of disentangling ourselves from each other's lives.

First, we vowed undying loyalty. *I will always remember you.* (To my horror, the first year after she left, I completely forgot her birthday.) Next, we untangled ourselves financially. I hated those complicated tax forms I had to fill out on her behalf, and I was thrilled to get rid of them. And finally, we promised to keep in touch.

Still, I was surprised at how little we saw of her after she left. You have to understand, my children had loved her, had cried when she left, and missed her a lot. Toward the end, though, they had begun to complain that she wouldn't let them grow up. "You're going to forget all about me," she once said plaintively to them. They didn't forget her, but, enthralled with their after-school daycare, they got on with the business of growing up.

After a few intermittent visits, almost two years went by without seeing her. Then, one Sunday last fall, Emily and I went shopping for her back-to-school clothes, and right in the middle of the Eaton Centre—a huge shopping mall—as we were going down the escalator, there, suddenly, on the up escalator, was Zusette with her two sisters. She looked at us, we looked at her, and we all waved frantically.

If this were fiction, the most poignant ending would be: "And we never saw her again." But it was real life, and Zusette quickly hopped on the down escalator and came back to meet us. She looked beautiful. She was in her second year of studying nursing—having apparently kissed her dreams of being a lawyer goodbye—and she seemed both happy and, for the first time, totally at ease with me. We both blurted out an apology at the same time for not having kept in touch, and we both said we'd call. Zusette wrote her new phone number on a scrap of paper and I put it in my purse. It's still there.

Standing there in the mall that day, I knew that our former relationship was over for good. She oohed and aahed over how much Emily (who shyly hung back a bit) had grown, and looked startled when I told her that Jonathan was almost as tall as she was now. We talked for a few minutes, and then she turned to go.

Holding Emily's hand, I watched her leave, but my mind was somewhere else. It had flown back in time, back to a familiar scene.

It is a weekday, around 5:30 PM Arriving home from work, I park the car and come in through the back-yard gate. I am able to catch a glimpse of the children through the sliding glass door before they can see me. They are sitting at the table with Zusette, hard at work doing cutouts or painting, or sometimes eating. And all three heads are bent in concentration, or thrown back in laughter. They look utterly rapt—and utterly happy. And looking at them, my heart is both full—and sore.

THE BRAIN OF A WORKING MOM

I love the phrase working mother, as if there were any other kind: anyone who is a mother works from the moment she opens her eyes in the morning to well beyond the sound of her children's lovely rhythmic breathing once they are fast asleep at night. But many of us do other work as well. And in order to do so, we sometimes have to be very secretive about who we really are, and what is really on our minds. That, in turn, triggers a modern condition known as The Secret Psychosis of Mothers with Jobs.

On a dramatic level, it works like this. Let's say you have a major project to finish at work that morning, or you're due at an important meeting, or you're covering someone else's shift. This happens, of course, to be the very day that your sitter announces she has to leave immediately because a relative she has never previously mentioned is on her deathbed; or the parents you carpool with all succumb to the flu, and expect you to drive four pre-schoolers to and from nursery school; or your own school-age child declares at the breakfast table that his stomach hurts really bad, and you have no daytime sitter.

The response to this turn of events is understandable panic (the Edvard Munch domestic scream) quickly followed by the most intensive telephone search ever conducted in a short period of time to find a solution to the problem. I have been on both ends of these phone calls—the mothers who phone, voices warbling, looking for help; the calls I've made, sounding as if I need to be sedated, asking for help, and believe me, begging is certainly not off-limits.

With my voice cracking, I have promised to do twice my share next time *if only someone will help me.* (It does help your credibility in these situations if you have managed, in the past, to do your share, a good thing to keep in mind.) What amazes me is that someone usually will help you out, and she has her own unbelievable saga of children to care for and deadlines to meet.

You might wonder what happens to husbands in all this *Sturm und Drang.* Well, the best I can say about them is, sometimes they are available, but most of the time, they have already left for a breakfast meeting. Mothers lead very different lives from fathers.

After you have found a solution that will not necessarily alarm the child welfare authorities, then comes the deception. You throw on your clothes, pinning that ripped hemline you forgot to sew, race to the meeting, pat down your hair, walk in—and knock 'em dead. And, unless you have a close confidante on hand, you usually make no mention of the catastrophe that you have just handled.

Most employers—and many colleagues—no matter how understanding, simply do not want to hear about the ongoing soap opera that is many a mother's life. Nor, professionally, is it considered a good idea to fill them in. (They might get the idea that having a home, a family, and a job is hard work.)

Even on a less dramatic, daily basis, our brains are constantly operating on two different levels at once: the professional task at hand (*Yes, Frank, let's put that issue on the table*), and whatever domestic problem needs an immediate solution—a child's Hallowe'en costume (*How do I make bunny ears?*), a birthday present that needs to be bought, or remembering that your daughter forgot to take her gym clothes.

Sometimes, one level leaks. (*Yes, Frank, let's put those bunny ears on the table.*) Once, during a political assignment I had undertaken, a pompous executive assistant informed me that the cabinet minister I was profiling was about to go into an important meeting, and that I should be there when she came out.

But I, obsessed with my son's rapidly approaching fifth birthday party, blurted out, "I'm sorry, I have to go to Toys 'R' Us." He stared at me with astonishment (or was it contempt?). I quickly recovered by telling him I was the president of Toys 'R' Us, but I'm not sure he believed me.

Of course, this split-brain syndrome happens because we deny that a large part of our lives is made up of mundane but incredibly important domestic tasks. In the end, the G-7 talks may take a back seat to whether there was enough construction paper on hand to start a school project that evening. Why should I feel any less intellectually gifted because I have to focus on that too?

In fact, perhaps working mothers are *more* gifted than other human beings—able to operate on two complex levels simultaneously *and* remember to bring home the makings for a chicken stir-fry.

Maybe we should donate our brains to science.

MEN: HOME A LOT, TOO

*C*amille Paglia, the provocative feminist scholar and writer who
has become the Andrew Dice Clay of feminism—a stand-up
scholar for our times—not too long ago told yet another sell-out
audience that, as a bisexual growing up, she had often wished fervently that she were a man. Now, she says, her biggest nightmare
would be to wake up and find she *is* a man. Why? Because men are
in need of approval all the time, and in reality are dominated by
women. You can see it at the malls, she cracked, the old guy shuf-
fling along and his wife at him: "No you *can't* have a hot dog!"

Like most of the audience, I was both horrified and amused, and
had to concede privately that I had force-marched my husband
through a few malls myself. But there is power, and then there is
Power. And anything you witness at the mall can be more than repli-
cated, with the roles reversed, in the boardroom and in the bedroom.

Paglia, a single woman who, by her own admission, is not dependent on men even for her sexual satisfaction, seems to have no
understanding at all of the extent of the power relationship between
men and women in all facets of daily life. Believe me, last time I
looked, men in suits still ruled the world. Yet, I have to admit that
men have never seemed so vulnerable, so in need of reassurance, as
they do today. It appears they are finally making changes in their

behaviour that no amount of prodding from feminists or male liberationists, no social pamphlet or panel show on modern men could have accomplished as quickly as that other great agent of social change—the economy.

The economy? In the midst of today's staggering unemployment rates and panicky economic climate, on the heels of one of the worst recessions in modern times, men are no longer able to count on what was always their greatest measure (well, apart from that other one) of self-worth: their ability to be successful, to prove themselves in the market economy, to provide.

Many a man has been shattered by the knowledge that, at least for the time being, he is not the major breadwinner in the home, and the balance of power between himself and his female partner has shifted dramatically as the woman continues to be employed while he is sidelined. You know this is happening because of the number of men you see at midday pushing strollers and picking up kids.

As a consequence, men are being forced into redefining themselves. When my husband's small investment business was hit by the last recession, I saw some changes in him. He was always focused on his family, but he used to be gone a lot in the evenings, doing deals, with a staggering (and swaggering, for that matter) degree of freedom, especially compared to my own highly scheduled existence: he walked out in the morning and came back in the evening when his last meeting was over, usually between eight and ten at night, when the air was thick with resentment.

There is a well-known syndrome (I invented it) called Re-entry Burn, in which many women admit their first reaction when their husbands walk through the door at night is an overwhelming desire to bash their heads in. You know, the "I've been here coping with screaming kids in the arsenic hour and you've managed to miss it all and come home when they're finally subdued and I'm exhausted" lament.

Now, like many men I've heard of, he's home a lot more—every night in fact—for dinner. There are fewer deals to be done, and no justification for expense-account dinners anyway. This change in the schedule led first to a few wry jokes: "Oh no, you're not coming home again tonight! That means I'll have to cook instead of inhaling whatever the kids are having." One friend of mine actually whispered into the phone one morning: "He's *still* here—I don't think there is anything to do at his office. What am I going to do?"

But despite the jokes, at our house we actually began to get into a smoother domestic rhythm, one that led to more intimacy—both between us, and between my husband and our children. "I feel almost organically connected to you and the kids," he said the other day, and I knew just what he meant. His presence in the evenings is steady now, whereas in the past it was unpredictable, and sometimes even jarring. In general, except of course for the relentless worry about how to survive the economic thrusts and parries, our life together feels warmer and better.

But what a trade-off. Does it really have to be an either/or situation—the pursuit of economic success versus real intimacy? Somehow, I think that once men really get a taste of the rewards of intimacy, they may never go back in that same ferociously driven way to the jungle again. In any event, there may not be much of a jungle to go back to.

TINY PERFECT POLICE

*W*e left a neighbourhood party the other day with our son in crusade mode, in the front seat of the car. "That is not a healthy household," he intoned. "They had nothing to eat in the kids' area except for ketchup chips and Cheezies." "Jonathan," I said wearily, "it was a party."

My daughter, five, and less vehement, I thought, than her brother, said to me with passionate force the other day, "Mommy, when I grow up, I hope I never pollute!" A crucial sentiment, I grant you, but I wondered about the ferocity and the self-condemnatory aspect of it. I got the impression she thought she was on the verge of becoming a very bad person, and further, that she felt she was surrounded on all sides by major sinners. This was confirmed to me when she came home from school the next day and said gravely, "Sally [the name has been changed to protect the innocent] gave me junk food at snack time!" You would have thought it was heroin she had been handed, instead of half a Twinkie.

I have, on more than one occasion, walked down the street with both of my kids and cringed when they have seen someone cycling slowly by without a helmet. Without any regard for extenuating circumstances (maybe the helmet was at the dry cleaners), not to mention privacy, they have said loudly to me, "Mom, did you see that,

that's terrible!" Then, before I can reply, "Well, yes he probably *would* be safer wearing a helmet, but let's not do a citizen's arrest here," they've already accosted the helmetless person: "Why aren't you wearing a helmet? It's not safe to ride a bike without one." Just in case the cyclist thinks I have anything to do with this roadside jury, I smile weakly and say, "They're very conscious of bicycle safety these days," but I feel embarrassed, for the cyclist and for us.

These are the days when I wonder whether we've gone too far in our zeal to make this planet a safer, healthier place. My children and their friends are so busy spouting slogans, prohibitions, and value judgments against polluters, smokers, unsafe bicycle riders, and eaters of junk food that I feel I'm living with the tiny perfect police.

The puritanical zeal with which my son dispatches smokers is almost as breathtaking as the weed itself. "This is a smoke-free zone," he has told many visitors to the house, adding, just to bring them to their knees, "Don't you know it's bad for you?" (At a slightly younger age, he outdid himself one day, combining his religious development with anti-smoking awareness, by asking, "Mom, why is smoking not good for the Jews?")

Was it something we said that has turned them into junior moralists, small insistent crusaders, unwilling to let a single slip— whether it's theirs, or someone else's—go by? I did a quick attitude check, starting with the junk food, and remembered, even though we are not nutritional saints around here, that I had come down a bit heavy on their father when he brought some nutritionally challenged baked goods into the house. And yes, I did make loud cluck clucking sounds when he spooned a huge mound of brown sugar into my daughter's porridge. But I don't *think* I came on like *Judgment at Nuremberg*.

I had one mother tell me she brought home a new coat with a soft plush collar only to have her daughter say pointedly, "I hope that's not *real* fur." It wasn't, but don't we need to lighten up a bit here?

We have talked to our children about litter and waste, about the value of saving, re-using, and simply not getting things we don't

need. We have shown them, by example rather than pronounce-
ment, that we don't throw away food, that we're careful with paper,
that we don't, you know, toss old chicken bones on the road. Isn't
that enough? Apparently not.

A group at my children's school is called The Environmental
Avengers. There is a zeal to all this that can too easily tip over into
self-righteousness, and a kind of not very attractive finger-wagging.
The finger-wagging can also, ludicrously, be carried over into a
wardrobe of tee-shirts that deliver mini-lectures—"SAVE THE
EARTHWORMS"—one for each day of the week.

Yet many passionate environmentalists respond that the time for
being nice is over—the earth is in such a mess, and polite calls for
change have not worked; so finger-wagging, at the very least, is
absolutely indicated. To many activists, our children are our only
hope. It is our children, of course, and their children who will be in
a worse mess than we are if we don't change our habits. The con-
tinuing depletion of the ozone layer, for instance, is a metaphor for
the end of childhood itself, or at least the childhood of playing outside on sunny, carefree days.

So I am thankful for the school system's anti-smoking, anti-drug,
and environmental campaigns. But there has got to be a way to help
young children sort out the delicate balance between individual lib-
erties and the greater good, to get the message across to them that
certain things are better—for the planet and for our bodies—without turning them into people who are intolerant of others, people
with a lack of empathy for human failings. People who can't enjoy
the occasional Cheezie. Tiny perfect police.

EACH SOLD SEPARATELY

*T*he first time I ever told my son, "We can't afford this," it was in a store, it was about a toy he desperately wanted, and I whispered the news to him, aware that I was violating some sacred baby-boom tenet: *thou shalt provide thy child with a mountain of loot, stuff he may play with only once or twice, but stuff he's gotta have.* He looked at me quizzically. He was only four then, and he had not yet heard about "affording" and "too expensive." Up until that point, his life and that of his little sister had been filled with pleasant, goodie-receiving experiences, with, so far as he knew, no price tag attached—presents on special occasions, treats when Daddy came home from a trip, or even when Daddy came home from the office. (I think there is a case to be made here for gender-linked behaviour; in most families I've canvassed, it is the father who buys spontaneously for the kids, not the mother.) And then there were treats on not so special occasions—a casual visit to the local bookstore, even a walk along the boardwalk, all seemed to result in *things.* Whatever happened to just memories?

But now I was signalling a change in the program, a slow-down in the acquisition stage. Was I trying to tell him we had lost the house in a poker game? Well, yes, in a metaphorical sense, we had. Like many others, we had been gambling on a buoyant economy. However, times were getting tougher, and we had no choice but to pare our spending down.

But it was more than that. I was appalled at the amount of toys they had. As one of my friends says, many modern homes look as though they have been decorated by Toys 'R' Us. Motorized teddy bears, half-built Lego sets, a musical angel that, when wound up, plays "Send in the Clowns," a matted stuffed cat that has kittens inside her Velcroed belly, a robot called My Pal, Too, which always looked, to me, anyway, like nobody's pal, and even a bit menacing as, depending on its battery power, it unpredictably lurched into action.

I factored the cost of them all against their transitory attraction, and it saddened me. Nor did it really console me that in comparison with some other children, our children's material goods seemed fairly modest. What bothered me was their blithe assumption that acquiring these things was an effortless activity. And the waiting period between wishing (out loud) and getting was immodestly short. (Not their fault, but ours.)

Those incessant television commercials issuing seductive come-ons ("Baby Alive!" "Cars That Change Color!") to the children became an increasing irritation. You know you are in trouble when your daughter's daily mantra is *each sold separately*.

Perhaps we were just in sync with society's changing mood (or deepening fears, or descending reality), but the "this-is-too-expensive-we-can't-afford-it" feeling caught on like wildfire with all of us. My husband refrained from buying his emotional hardware—you know, electronic gizmos like portable phones that keep men happy for at least a week, I retired all but one credit card, and the children began examining heads of lettuce in the grocery store, wondering aloud if we could afford them.

Fiscal restraint, however, did not occur to them at the check-out counter as they eyed those chocolate bars. All grocery stores employ a secret tactic called the Smarties Manoeuvre. This involves placing large quantities of candy for sale by the cashier, which is of course where, after a long, arduous shop during which one child has dropped a tub of cottage cheese all over the floor while another has rammed the cart into the backside of a very shaky senior citizen, the parent with them is usually ready to lie down in the aisle and sob. What's a box of Smarties compared to a full nervous breakdown?

Give or take a few boxes of Smarties, we stayed on our modest fiscal course, with a few bumpy moments along the way. There was the time we were in a mall, and I said yes they could ride the mechanized cars, only to find out that the operator wanted $2 per ride. So I reneged, and had to deal with two kids going loudly non-linear while the ride operator smirked at me. (His smile said it all—too bad lady, I'm a witness and you said yes.) I held my tenuous moral ground—the value of a promise vs. my too-much-money stand— and found a merry-go-round for twenty-five cents. And a fairly subdued carousel ride it was. (I always used to think that when my kids melted down in a public place, everyone was staring and pointing and clucking their tongues, that soon the store management would send along a photographer to get our mug shots so we'd never be allowed in the vicinity again. But now I know that only some people are looking at us with disdain, while the rest feel pity, and deep gratitude that it is not their child lying in the aisle, banging her head and yelling, "I want it I want it I want it!")

Of course, our parents, who didn't know from Toys 'R' Us, smile in a superior way at our newfound restraint, and say, "What took you so long? You're just doing your job as a parent, teaching them values." But I'm excited. We're on a roll! Next stop, the disadvantaged. After that, peer pressure.

In our household, we now have values. Each sold separately.

BIRTHDAY MADNESS

*W*hen they get the time capsule ready for our generation, among the most embarrassing artifacts to be included will be the quintessential video of the elaborate kids' birthday parties we staged. Leaving aside the questionable practice of compulsive videotaping, we will have a lot to explain. Watch while the children sit glassy-eyed as Bonzella, the hired ($50 an hour) clown/singer/magician/balloon artist, gives a barely adequate performance that pales in comparison with what they see on television every day of the week! View entire tables of unruly children consuming expensive junk food at restaurants and bowling alleys with criminal noise levels while anxious parents wait for the bill! Observe the little guests looking truly attentive only when it's time to pick up their aptly named loot bags on which parents collectively spent what amounts to the GNP of at least one Third World country for instantly forgettable junk and candy that were, in effect, payments for each greedy guest! Can we really come up with a decent explanation for all this?

Birthday madness is looming yet again on our own domestic horizon as we head into (the horror! the horror!) two birthday parties, six weeks apart, both of which have been under endless discussion ever since we tore down the streamers from last year's extravaganzas. It usually comes over my children just as they are being tucked into bed, this desire to yet again revise the "theme" of their upcoming party, as in "Mom, I've changed my mind, I don't want a bowling party, I want a swimming party with all my friends in the deep end." (This when she was four, and did not yet swim.)

Let's face it, apart from Hallowe'en and the Christmas/Chanukah season, no other event looms as all-important in a child's year as his or her birthday. That should never change. Birthdays are a wonderful time to affirm how special a child is. But did we really need to hire tea-leaf readers/dance instructors/pullers-of-scared-rabbits-out-of-hats to prove it? What, they couldn't play pin-the-tail-on-the-donkey like the rest of us did?

Oh, it's so complicated, like everything else this smart, well-educated, well-meaning, but pathologically zealous generation of parents has tried to do: we wanted to give them the *best*, the very best, but didn't we realize that catered parties for four-year-olds were a sin against common sense? I have been to a few, as a friendly helping hand, and my heart has gone out to the birthday child's parents—who, after all, only wanted to present their child with a magic moment or two. But no child, having their druthers, would want to sit in a restaurant for an hour and wait for a plate of chicken fingers to come. This is a party? No, this is a cholesterol-laden armed robbery of their right to a childhood.

I know there are extenuating circumstances. Working parents are stretched, and sometimes it is easier to let one of these hyperactive, child-oriented restaurants do the job. (My idea of Hell would definitely feature a Chuck E Cheese ambience.) Besides, these places are open on Sundays, which is when more and more children's parties are taking place. Who can get it together by Saturday these days?

I am not quarrelling, either, with creative, even fanciful house parties for kids. These are not new. My husband grew up in a household where theme parties rolled out of his mother's hip pocket like so many pennies. I did not, and frankly I have never once, even in deep therapy, suddenly realized that what my childhood lacked was a theme. The only advantage he has is an innate ability to come up with, in short order, anything from a hand-painted and ketchup-smeared (pirate's blood) treasure map to 101 ways to hang streamers.

The truth is, the more elaborate and structured a child's party is, the less fun it will be for the kids. I once overproduced what I thought was going to be a brilliant party for my daughter's sixth birthday—an old-fashioned tea party in which the girls were asked to come in their mothers' dresses. I fussed over the table, I spent time and money I shouldn't have on props (well, lace doilies), and I watched the little girls in high heels hobble in, one of them dressed alarmingly in a black cocktail outfit. But what I noticed, with a sinking feeling, was that the girls weren't having a barrel of laughs, which probably speaks to the strictures of fancy dresses and lace doilies, as much as to overweaning parental involvement. It was only when they kicked off their heels, stripped off their dresses, and pared down to their shorts that the party began to feel like a good time. Ironically, even the pictures didn't turn out.

As for boys' parties, well, the only piece of wisdom I can impart here is, when they are served their food, either leave the room or gag. And the older they get, the more creatively nauseating they become. Our son's birthday is in May, so it was no problem last year to wait out on the front porch while one of his friends won the belching contest by burping out the entire alphabet song before he fell off his chair, lay on the floor, and yelled, "I'm gonna barf!" One more reason to avoid using a video camera.

When it comes to birthday parties these days, kids are getting as jaded as that Cole Porter heroine singing "I get no kick from champagne." You don't believe me? Another birthday invitation arrived the other day for my daughter. "Oh no," she sighed. "Not another restaurant party!"

Quick. Get out the musical chairs, make a jug of Kool-Aid, and add this message to the time capsule: "We are truly sorry for our sins."

FEMINIST TIPS FOR GIRLS

I have three enduring images of my daughter so far in her tender journey into little girlhood. One was at two-and-a-half, when I first took her to preschool. With the face of an angel and the short, spikey haircut of a punker, she corrected the teacher when she was introduced as Emily. "I not Emily, I Captain Hook," she growled. Good, I thought secretly, she's got attitude. Better a pirate than a princess.

But at three, the attitude was a little too much for me as she lay down on the floor and stubbornly refused to wear an exquisite flowered dress for her birthday party. That dress was perfect, how could she not love it? Somehow, I failed to grasp the irony of the moment. Here I was, hoist on my own manifesto, pleading with my daughter to wear the ultimate in gender typecasting. (You can always tell the daughters of feminists, someone once sardonically told me, they're the ones in head-to-toe pink.)

After her refusal to wear dresses, I stocked up on leggings, just in time for her to change her mind and insist on flounces every day, not just for her but for me. Now there was a challenge. "Mommy," she said authoritatively in my bedroom one morning, "you can't be pretty if you don't wear a skirt." I, who live in jeans and leggings, felt a momentary stab of regret at having failed her in the image department.

Ruefully remembering that flowered dress, I understood then we were even in the disappointment department, and that it would not be the last time either of us would fail to live up to the other's expectations.

My most recent image of her is enshrined in a photograph that always stops me in my tracks when I walk by it at home. It is of Emily, not quite five, accepting a bouquet of flowers from us after her first ballet recital. Her back is perfectly straight, the smile is transcendent, but what strikes me most is her poise and the level gaze in her eyes. There is not a hint of coyness there.

Emily is turning six this month. Her hair has grown long, and she has acquired certain girlish mannerisms almost by osmosis. I narrow my eyes and wonder, how does she *know* to take the scarf she found in my drawer and wind it about her chest in a daring bandeau top? Where did she learn to flirt with the men and be more direct with the women? I watch anxiously for signs of her spirit being tamed. Is there too much capitulation to her older brother? Is she facilitating his needs at the expense of her own?

Watching her, bent in concentration over her meticulous art work, or out joyously playing baseball with her father and brother in the back alley, I find it inconceivable that her desires or dreams could be thwarted one day simply because she is female.

But I'm vigilant, just the same. One time, I bristle when my mother innocently praises her "good little" housekeeping skills. And when she requests *Sleeping Beauty* as her bedtime story, I ask her if she isn't tired of the princess always being rescued by the prince, and could it not be the other way around?

On the whole, I find myself comfortable with these smaller gestures, unable yet to be overtly didactic with this wonder unfolding in front of my eyes. But perhaps, to some, this *is* overt didacticism. To me, however, after twenty years of avid feminism, it is subtle. I've made my stands—marched for abortion rights (and would do so again) so that she would never, ever have to continue with an unwanted pregnancy, written angry, anguished articles, succumbing to a few excesses along the way.

And I suppose I stand before her, a product of all this foment—
a wife who loves her husband, but still snaps at him when he does
not do his share of the housework. A mother who cooks, cleans,
and looks after her, but also has her other important work. A
woman who, like her mother before her, almost never leaves the
house without first putting on her lipstick.

I cannot control her impressions of me, and sharp-eyed as she is,
she will pick up on the ambiguities that are there. My daughter will
have to make her own journey to womanhood, and I won't know
until she gets there what she deemed necessary for the trip and
what she decided to leave behind. I have a feeling though, it will
not be her attitude or her lipstick.

IN OUR HOUSEHOLD, ILLNESS IS NOT A METAPHOR

*I*t's time for that family game known as germ roulette. One child is at school, the other happy with the sitter, I'm in my office, dressed up for a change (well, I needed one silk shirt anyway). I'm looking forward to a business lunch (part-time working mothers actually do look forward to business lunches; it's the only time they don't have to carry a wad of paper napkins to the table to wipe up spills). Suddenly, the phone rings. It's Zusette, our baby-sitter: "Emily seems sick. She says her tummy hurts, and she's pale." My heart sinks. I hesitate only a fraction of a second and then make the decision to leave the office and drive the fifteen minutes home. Zusette would not be calling me unless she thought it was serious. (On the other hand, the last time I got such a phone call and left work, it was to pick up Emily at preschool, where the teachers swore she was ill; when we got in the car, I asked her what didn't feel good. "My skirt," was her reply.)

This time, I arrive to find a truly listless child who is only able to say her tummy does hurt. I get a rush doctor's appointment, cancel my lunch date, and start down the steps of the house with my daughter in my arms, thinking in terms of medical headlines—Acute Appendicitis, Stomach Blockage, Gastroenteritis.

Just as I get to the car, whoops, she throws up. And up and up and up. She feels a lot better. My shirt, however, is in critical condition. We run back into the house to change. I decide to go through with the doctor's appointment anyway, where the doctor (putting an additional monetary strain on an already beleaguered medical system) confirms, yup, she needed to throw up and now she seems okay. I feel sheepish.

Back in the car, Emily chats merrily all the way home. I tuck her into a corner of the couch, and then leave her in Zusette's capable hands. It's been two hours and twenty minutes, but it seems like an eternity. Back I go to work, where I grab a sandwich and spend the next hour worrying about her anyway. There is no immediate return from . . . the illness zone.

Illness is the wild card in a heroic attempt to have an orderly life. If the children are off school, and no alternative arrangement can be made, then one parent—in our case, usually the mother but more and more often nowadays the father—is off work too. Or, if she works at home, she is held hostage on her couch, sometimes for weeks, with germs circulating in the overheated air like so many guerrilla fighters and children clinging to her. And unless she has help in the daytime, there is no way, without taking her sick children with her, to even leave to get a prescription filled, let alone regain her sanity with a breath of fresh air.

So she sits there, eyes glazed over after one too many games of Guess Who? And just as she's gratefully watching her child bounce back, *she* gets sick, closely followed by that most mutant of all male species . . . The Sick Husband.

May I present a typical family medical dossier, The Sore Throat: His, Hers, and Theirs. Hers: Gee, I know my throat is scratchy and I'm as tired as hell, but if I can just get dinner on the table and then put my feet up, I'll be fine for the school field trip tomorrow. His (his voice reduced to a theatrical whisper): I *think* I'll be all right, I just have to lie down right now. I've told the office I won't be back till I'm able to talk on the phone, so I'll just catch forty winks—any new magazines come today?" And Theirs: "Mommy! Whaa! More juice! Why does my throat hurt? Will you play Junior Scrabble again? I'm bored. Why won't you watch *The Lion King* with me for the third time?" . . . and, well, you get the picture.

Of course, there is a sneaky psychological up side to this. Taking care of a sick child is, perversely, everything motherhood was cracked up to be and more. In a job where there is no such thing as closure, you truly can make a difference, applying cold cloths to a feverish little forehead, measuring out the antibiotic with the brisk efficiency of a ward nurse, letting him have two popsicles in a row, reading a book and snuggling as you wait for the children's Tylenol to take effect.

Germ roulette also gives you the chance to win the Nobel Prize for Overfunctioning. Once, while my mother lay critically ill in the hospital, I had my own immediate family members throwing up on every floor of the house, stricken simultaneously by a malevolent flu. I remember rushing from the baby to my husband to my son, panting with exhaustion, basins and towels at the ready, thermometer in my pocket, all the while worrying about my mother, and thinking: "You've got to be kidding." But also, let's face it, imagining myself as . . . Iron Woman. By the time my sister-in-law arrived, however, bearing chicken soup and sympathy, I had devolved into Irony Woman, wondering whether Susan Sontag was living alone when she wrote illness was a metaphor.

There is nothing more wrenching than the sight of a pale, sick, listless child. Often, I've been surprised and stirred by a flash of bravery or fortitude that even adults fail to reveal in the face of a bad flu or cold. Still, I find myself praying for the return of robust obnoxiousness as I watch my little patient lolling about on the couch. My own head feels pretty heavy too, come to think of it. I lie back in a bittersweet surrender to the moment . . . .

But things better be back to normal by tomorrow.

INTENSIVE CARE

*I*t has been almost eight years, but I can still remember the smell of the intensive care unit, slightly chemical and at the same time sweet. And the surreal, time-out-of-time quality of the waiting room, with its dreary walls and drab furniture. I spent literally weeks in that room, convinced that if I sat there, my mother would not die. I remember, too, the technical jargon we tossed around as if we'd been to medical school—"And how are her blood gases today, doctor?" Most of all, I remember the creepy whooshing and pumping sound of the respirator, the strongest they had, pumping 100 breaths a minute into her body, breathing for her, as she lay motionless on a hospital bed.

My mother had called me one winter morning, out of breath, to say, "I think I need to go to the hospital." Usually robust and lively, she had had a cold that had gone on too long, a bad cough, and suddenly she was not up to even simple tasks.

I was petrified when I went to get her. It was the first time I had really faced her fragility. We are very close—we see each other once a week, speak on the telephone nearly every day. She is the only person I know whose day I can interrupt with some vital piece of trivia about the children and get a truly attentive response. Some people have been dazzled by her ladylike qualities, but lurking underneath that graciousness is more tenacity than meets the eye. Moreover, she can recount, in highly amusing detail, who said what on CNN last night. My mother, the media maven.

At the hospital, the world shifted terrifyingly on its axis, from mother-with-a-slight-breathing-problem to, within two days, a mother unconscious in intensive care. She had a viral pneumonia that was not responding to treatment; her lungs were filling with fluid. A young resident gathered us together in another drab room and told us she could die that night. He said they would try but . . . .

She did not die that night, or the next night or the next one after that. She stayed alive—but barely. Despite our terror, we swung into high gear. My sister-in-law, whose social skills are formidable, took on the nurses, praising them, joking with them, but also letting them know that the patient in the bed by the window was someone special. My brother and I, usually no paragons of tact, summoned enough of it to question, question, and question again the doctors who came to treat her—and not get thrown out in the process. *How is she today, what treatment are you pursuing, what difference will it make, what can we do?*

A month of questions went by. In the waiting room, I cried along with the relatives of other dying patients. The outside world seemed more foreign to me than that place. What kept us there, apart from the love, was the struggle itself between life and death, so compelling it made even our children and their daily lives seem remote.

What would we have done, my sister-in-law and I, if we had not had neighbours, friends, and relatives to help care for our children? What would we have done if, like so many other women on whom the burden falls to care for the sick, we had had to go to outside jobs that winter? We joked that this was our job.

Our husbands came and went, but the two of us, sweatsuit-clad Lady Macbeths wringing our hands (but armed with good hand lotion), sat constant vigil. Sometimes we cried, other times we lapsed into tasteless humour and uncontrollable laughter, which brought us back to tears again.

For well over a month, my mother never really regained full consciousness. We all felt slightly silly talking to her lifeless form, but we did. "Hi Mom, it's snowing outside, and Jonathan has a bad cold . . ."

One day, I saw the head of the unit obliterate her chances of survival with one dismissive sweep of his arm, as he stood with a group of residents around her bed. "No progress, nothing," he said gruffly. Standing off to one side, unnoticed, I was sickened. Hadn't the respirologist, who had devoted so much time to her, just told us that she had shown some improvement? But this doctor disagreed: "The chances are that she will not survive, and if she does, she will be tied to a respirator for the rest of her life."

That night, my brother and I, slightly deranged, drove around the hospital parking lot arguing about whether to have an open or closed casket. The next day, absurdly, we were back cheerleading at her bedside: "Hi Mom . . ."

Then, as suddenly and mysteriously as she had gotten ill, she began to recover. My mother, the miracle patient. The day she was released from hospital, I ran into the head of the unit (whom we had, in the interim, renamed Dr. Death). "Okay, so I was wrong," he said, throwing his hands up in mock horror. "I'm human too."

I wondered if he had learned his lesson, and if I had learned mine. His lesson had to do with the inflexible dogmatism with which he had presented his view. What if we had believed him and given up on her? What if we had concluded, like one of those dedicated nurses, that it was hopeless? This nurse confessed to us later that, despite her vigorous care of her patient, she used to come in on her shift, stare at my mother, and say to herself, "Now why are they keeping this poor woman alive?"

My lessons were equally profound, and are reinforced every time my mother arrives at our house, looking wonderful and summoning up considerable energy to be with her grandchildren. (She now uses some of that energy to do volunteer work with anxious families in the very waiting room that consumed our lives.)

I learned that the human body can sustain unimaginable trauma, and still become whole again. I learned that when doctors tell you someone you love is dying, you must not always believe them. You must fight for their lives. And most importantly of all, I learned that my mother is a remarkable woman.

NANNY

*W*hen you marry into a family, you acquire relatives you never dreamed of having. When I first met my husband, I took a deep breath when I realized he came equipped with a formidable mother whose organizing impetus would give most world leaders a run for their money, an emotional father with an emotional temper to match, and three intense and creative siblings, not to mention their intense and creative partners. As they say in Hebrew, *dayenu*, that would have been enough.

But no, there was one more relative to consider, perhaps the most important of all. She was my husband's grandmother, his mother's mother, but everyone called her Nanny. As a young woman, Nanny was a party girl—and a whiz at cards. Raised in a close Jewish family, with a passel of musical brothers and sisters, she loved to dance, sing, and play the night away.

By the time I met her, she was a matriarch, able to look back on many joys and sorrows. She got married at her dying mother's bedside. In early marriage, she buried her little daughter. Her husband died when she was in her fifties. And now she was an aging mother who fretted over her two adult children, a grandmother who thought it was her duty to stay up all night overseeing the lives of her eight grown grandchildren. Trouble was, as she saw it (usually around 4 AM), they kept making these *mistakes*.

And in Nanny's eyes, I was a whopper. She thought her grandson was doing a Very Bad Thing by falling in love with me, a non-Jewish woman (nothing personal, she assured me), and that wasn't my only flaw: "I always thought Martin wanted to marry someone tall," she moaned to me one day in her Tallullah Bankhead voice. I could see I was up against a piece of work.

Fortunately, my husband knew his own heart and mind. As for me, after much thought and a year-long conversion course (and with the help of slightly higher heels), I eventually became a reasonably tall Jewish bride. Nanny even danced at our wedding. Still, there were ruffled feathers to be smoothed. Nanny felt her beloved grandson had become distant, and complained vociferously about it—to me! I remember standing in an airport phone booth, having a phone conversation with her that felt like a scene in a movie, telling her she had forced him to choose between us, and he had chosen me.

Soon, however, the birth of our children made all this seem like ancient histrionics. Nanny immediately became a central and important fixture in their lives and in mine, dispensing advice and yes, criticism, but magically connecting with them, and through them, with me.

When did I begin to feel this enormous amount of affection for her? Was it when I saw her coo to my babies and dance them around the sunporch at the cottage? Or when I found myself secretly looking forward to sitting down beside her on the sofa for her next lecture in a series loosely entitled How To Keep Your Husband Happy? (Sample: "If he gets mad, don't you get mad in return. You wait till he cools down and then you talk to him.") With Nanny, the onus was always on the wife to placate, to please, to be there if needed. With Nanny, what you got was Tradition with a capital *T*.

And yet on some matters, she was surprisingly up to date. An early devotee of Phil Donahue, I suspect she knew more about cross-dressing fathers than the rest of us. Shlock sociology aside, you could also talk to her about politics and receive an astute reply.

But she was losing her sight—except, of course, she could still spot a crooked hemline at fifty paces—and she was tremendously frustrated. We all took turns saying, "Now, Nanny, it could be worse. At least you've still got that razor-sharp mind." She pretended to agree, but remained furious about her dimming universe.

The trouble, you see, with getting older is that it never, after a certain age, gets better again. When Nanny turned ninety-six, we celebrated her long life—but not her daily life. She was getting frailer and more fatigued by the day. All her siblings and her friends had died. Her generation had moved on. The party girl wanted to go home.

Not too long before she died, she talked to me about how far she had come, to accept so much change and the modern behaviour of her grandchildren. "It hasn't been easy, you know," she said, as if both congratulating herself and acknowledging the reality around her.

I couldn't help thinking how far I had come as well over the past thirteen years. I thought back to my initial alarm, wondering, whatever am I going to do with this woman?

The answer it seems, was simple: love her.

*   *   *

We buried Nanny in the pouring rain, while my mother-in-law and her brother threw handfuls of dirt on the coffin, and the centuries-old Jewish prayer of mourning, Kaddish, was recited. Nine months later, we were back at her gravesite for the unveiling of her monument, but this time it was an exquisite fall morning, bright and sunny and filled to the brim with all the usual components of an extended family get-together—tension, laughter, sadness, memory, and hope. And some new components, too. What would Miss Manners have had to say about the two young girls—cousins, soul-mates, partners in crime—dressed in their best outfits if not their best behaviour, who giggled inappropriately all through the service, and moreover were catching mysterious, tiny little flies (vigorously!) at their great-grandmother's unveiling?

Never mind, those two young girls also had—and will have for-ever—vivid memories of Nanny, of who she was in relation to them, of the *challah* bread she baked on the Sabbath, the music she loved (Louis Armstrong singing "What a Wonderful World"), the way her raspy voice sounded on the phone when they would call her with some earth-shattering news of the day, and she would respond, "Aw, go on!"

At the unveiling, I was standing on a slight incline, a little too far from those giggling girls to, ah, modify their behaviour with my highly perfected, but silent "If you continue to do this you will be sorry for the rest of your lives" gaze.

Later, we all laughed about the girls, and said Nanny would have gotten the joke. As we began the long drive back to Toronto from Montreal, I told one of the two gigglers and her brother how lucky they were to have had a close relationship with a great-grand-mother. Many of their friends don't even have a full set of grand-parents in their lives. But they got to know her, love her, miss her, and remember her. Goodbye Nanny, no flies on you.

"ARE YOU JEWISH OR CHRISTMAS?"

*O*ur son, in what we now refer to as his High Dogma period, used to greet people at the door in December by asking them, "Are you Jewish or Christmas?" Most people would laugh and readily answer, but I knew it was not a laughing matter for him. He was struggling to work out his own identity in a world gone crazy with tinsel and holly and ho ho ho.

Watching him, I would be aware of my own deep ambivalence on the subject of Christmas. I was brought up in a household that did not stress religion, but I did go to an Anglican Church Sunday school, and eventually, I belonged to a United Church group. There were many things I thought I might be when I grew up, but none of them was Jewish.

However, fate had a different spiritual agenda for me, and I fell in love with a Jewish man. We spent two agonizing years trying to reconcile our religious differences, which turned out to be not so much about religion, but about culture. As a member of the majority culture, it seemed to me at the time that converting to Judaism was something I could manage, especially because it wasn't religion he wanted so much as a Jewish home.

And so I promised, under the *chuppah*, to run a Jewish home, and

I've done so ever since. Oh, there was the matter of Christmas, but Christmas had, for a variety of emotional reasons, never been my favourite holiday. So even when a well-meaning but persistent relative of my husband's followed me from room to room pointing out that I would not be able to have a Christmas tree, I thought, on the whole, it was something I could live without. Pitch the tree. Deep-six the tinsel. Hold the holly.

But still, this season brings on the blues. How can it not? Every radio station blares Christmas music, every store sighs its commercial come-on, and every time we go anywhere—in an elevator, on a street, in a mall—my children are asked by people who don't know them, "What's Santa bringing you for Christmas?"

At first, I used to intervene hurriedly on their behalf, saying politely, "We celebrate Chanukah," but now I wait to see what they will come up with. It isn't easy. Sometimes my son mentions Chanukah and the fact that he is Jewish, and sometimes he gets overwhelmed, even angry. Once, he walked into a doctor's office, looked at the decorated tree, and said in a loud voice, the smallest Scrooge in captivity, "I hate Christmas!" An elderly woman turned around and looked at him in astonishment: What? A child hating Christmas?

But it is a legitimate response to an overwhelming ethos, and sometimes I, too, feel angry and overwhelmed in the face of it. To be fair, the schools have tried to right the balance, including Chanukah and other festivals in their curricula, but in doing so, they have given perhaps too much emphasis to Chanukah. It is a minor festival, marked by the lighting of the menorah, the eating of potato pancakes (latkes), and the giving of small presents to children, and it should not be pumped up to compete as a Jewish Christmas.

I watch with envy as my husband takes what he wants out of the Christmas season (the music, the good will, the egg nog) and leaves the rest of it (the store line-ups, the pressure to buy buy buy, and the holiday angst) blissfully behind.

Meanwhile, I keep thinking of our staircase. Sometimes I've wondered, in a secret, fleeting nostalgia for something I never really experienced (we didn't have a staircase when I was a child), what it would be like for my children to creep down the stairs, the banister wrapped in holly, and rush to their stockings hung on the mantel, or to a tree bulging with presents. I understand that this is a fantasy I am invoking, not memories of my own childhood, but rather an idealized, Norman Rockwell version of Christmas that many people who celebrate Christmas long for as well. But it is one thing to understand it, and quite another to let it go.

My children are pretty comfortable being Jewish. It's all they've ever known, after all. Despite all the adults walking around wringing their hands over mixed marriages and wondering if the children will be confused, the children are never as confused as we are. It is adults who turn religious differences into wars and family crises. When we go to my brother's, as we do each year for dinner on Christmas Day, my children accept in a way I never will that it is a nice holiday, but it is not theirs.

Besides, by then we have usually had our own celebration—a wonderful Chanukah party with dozens of latkes that we spent a whole afternoon making ahead of time, and all our friends and relatives, "Jewish or Christmas," joining with us as we light the menorah and sing the blessings. As we do, I always cry. And I try not to look at the staircase.

OH GOD, AND OTHER TALES
OF ENLIGHTENMENT

*O*ur children know who Jean Chrétien is, they know who Jim Carrey is, they know who Michael Jackson, Céline Dion, and Batman are, they even know who Louis Armstrong is, or was. But they don't really know who God is. It is a thought that is with me these days, as we approach The Season of Crumpled Wrapping Paper.

I used to read about "a Godless home" and feel as though I were reading about a very bad place, where people did very bad things. But in a sense, our home is Godless: we make no overt mention of a Supreme Being, we have never sat down with our children and handed them a set of religious beliefs, we don't pray. In our household, "God" is what you exclaim when you read a really weird story in the morning newspaper.

Indeed, we are, like many others, a family that has found a way to be Jewish without being particularly religious. We may light the candles for Shabbas every Friday night, and sing the blessings, but we don't do it to invoke belief in a divine power, we do it as a family-oriented cultural moment.

And because those blessings, whether for Friday nights or even for Chanukah, are performed in Hebrew, our children, who sing them beautifully, do not connect them precisely with God, and we do not overtly encourage them to do so. Call us practising hypocrites.

Without explicitly comparing notes, my husband and I have come to believe less, not more, in anything that organized religion has to offer. And while our collective conscience tells us we should be getting involved in synagogue life, our mutual instincts make us shy away from any institutionalized set of beliefs, any commitment to religious life.

And yet. Our children mention God to us more times than you would expect. Banned from the classroom, He still makes guest appearances in schoolyard mythology, along with Batman, Captain Spock, and any member of the Toronto Blue Jays. Or, like many children I'm aware of, they have heard about God from their baby-sitter, who is Catholic. She had her own highly developed sense of Him, one that I did not mind her discussing with our children. I refuse to close down the portals of their minds, to give them the idea that there is one shining way of truth and light and it runs through our household.

So when my children tell me God is watching, or that little children who die become angels in heaven, or that God can make something marvellous happen, I gently remind them that some people believe this but not everyone. I tell them that for other people, including me, God is more of a feeling and less of an actual presence. But they want gritty biographical details. Does He speak French or English? Did He really make it rain on my birthday? Could God be a girl? I try to tell them, when they bring these beliefs to me, what Jewish people believe, but even then I start splitting Talmudic hairs, getting down to what some Jews, as opposed to all Jews, believe. Being spiritually correct these days is as exhausting as being politically correct.

During the holiday season last year, our daughter was more obsessed with making sure the department store Santa, whom she visited with her class, did not find out she was Jewish than with what God was up to. I told her, be proud you're Jewish, but if you think you have to 'fess up to every guy in a red suit with a beard that you're not one of his regular customers, forget it. Relax. No one's going to sue you for sitting on his lap.

Our son, meanwhile, still fascinated by the fact that I converted from Christianity to Judaism after I met their father, occasionally asks, "Mom, what was it like, being a Christian?" making me feel a bit like Mel Brooks' one-thousand-year-old-man.

"Well," I pause, getting ready to launch into a serious discussion of what I believe now, as opposed to what I believed then, when suddenly it occurs to me that what he really wants to know is did I get more presents when I was Christian?

I reassure him that eight solid days of Chanukah gift-giving are nothing to sneeze at, and anyway this is not a contest. Or, for him, a choice. He is what he is (which is one of the main reasons I converted in the first place).

In the meantime, I constantly review my own set of beliefs, in preparation for a more intense level of questioning. Let me see, I believe in, among other things . . . divine retribution, being spiritual without being religious, intuition, being good but not necessarily being nice, fate, the redemptive power of love, God: the feeling, and definitely Louis Armstrong: the man.

Oh, and I absolutely believe in a white Christmas. It is the only white thing left that is spiritually, politically, and culturally correct.

CROSSING OVER

*W*hen I was a little girl of six or seven, my father took me to meet a friend of his at a country club whose members were predominantly Jewish. Coming out of the pool dripping wet, I ran into a classmate who expressed surprise to find me at her club, and told me with pride about its affiliation. Notwithstanding the fact that I was already a regular at an Anglican Sunday school, I ran down the length of the pool to my father, shouting, "Daddy, are I Jewish?" The people lounging poolside laughed indulgently. And having cleared up that little spiritual issue, I went on to have a good time in the pool.

The matter didn't come up again until I was thirty, and met the man of my dreams—a guy who told me that he considered himself to be "one of the world's few joyful Jews." He wooed me with Montreal bagels, legs that looked amazing in shorts, and some creatively wishful thinking. Early on, when I still could conceivably have bailed out, I asked him if his parents would mind that I wasn't Jewish. "Not really," he said. He must have liked my legs too.

Shortly after it became alarmingly clear to both of us that we just might end up spending our lives together, we embarked on a wrenching debate about whether I, being a lacklustre Protestant, could possibly convert to Judaism. Whatever family concerns had arisen about our plans were not, in the end, as important as our own: He—"I don't want to wake up at forty and find I've denied my cultural roots." Me— "I can't figure out if this is a feminist issue, an identity issue, or a religious issue. All I know is I'm not sure what I believe in any more."

Eventually, after a year-long study course for both of us, I found that I believed enough—just enough—to convert to reform Judaism. That was twelve years ago, and a cousin of my husband recently said warmly to me, "You're the most well-adjusted convert I've ever met."

Am I? Most of the time, it feels as though I have made the cultural leap. I've always had schmooze-ability. And apart from one disastrous *faux pas*, I seem to have mastered the language: You don't give a party, you *make* a party; you don't directly answer a question, you reply with another question. For example, the Jewish response to the profound question: "Are you happy?" is "What's not to be happy about?"

On the other hand, I have contravened some major cultural laws. I still slightly mispronounce the word "bubby"—can't get that "u" right—and I certainly could have been, on more than one occasion, charged and convicted under the Empty Fridge Act. Moreover, I refuse to pretend that I've always been Jewish, and in fact sometimes like to hold family dinner tables hostage with my "Back when I was Christian" reverie.

My conversion still seems remarkable to me. I was one thing for so many years, and then I became another. I went from being part of the majority culture, unthinkingly accepting its privileges, to being a member of a minority that, despite its accomplishments, despite its triumphs, has a history of persecution and rejection. I "crossed over," as a friend once laughingly said to me, and now I watch alertly from the other side. When it comes to anti-Semitism, both my head and my heart feel Jewish. I am prodigious at sniffing it out—perhaps because, to some of the ignorant, I go undercover. And I'm getting better at confronting it in all its varied guises: there are no Jewish princess jokes welcome here.

Growing up, I was educated in North American schools that, unlike many schools today, did little in the fifties and sixties to

enlighten the mainstream about other religious and cultural prac-
tices. I emerged from this system (and from my own home life) as an
adult with a generous capacity for tolerance, but a profound ignorance of what I was tolerating. That ignorance led me to my inglori-
ous *faux pas*: Soon after meeting my husband-to-be, I found myself at
a Jewish funeral. Turning to a friend, I whispered loudly, "I think the
Jewish funeral custom of sitting *shikse* is a wonderful one, don't you?"
(Of course, I meant sitting *shiva*—the traditional seven-day period of
mourning; *shikse* is the Yiddish word for a non-Jewish woman.)

Since then, sitting or standing, I have drawn much spiritual and
emotional strength from being Jewish. There is the perfection of
starting the new year in the fall, my favourite season, the joyful
singing around the seder table at Passover, the passionate attachment
Jews have to history, to the narrative—we are obligated, every
Passover, to retell the story of the exodus from Egypt, and it is a very
good story indeed. Judaism, it seems to me, is a religion made for a
writer. As American author Cynthia Ozick said, when asked how her
Jewishness affected her writing, "To be Jewish is to be a member of a
civilization with a long, long history . . . a procession of ideas."

On a more prosaic level, being Jewish also means being part of a
very reactive community: when there is a death, an illness, or a
blessing you jump right in, which suits me fine.

I am also in love with the Jewish insistence on the primacy of life
over death, but even after twelve years, I'm not too sure I understand the ingenious Book of Life arrangement. Jews believe that
every year at Rosh Hashanah, you are either "written down in the
Book of Life" for another year or you're not, which, to put it bluntly,
means that if you're not, come next year, you'll be dead. Moreover,
whether you live or die does not depend (to my great relief) on how
sinful you are, but you also can't squeak by on a technicality, there's
no maître d' you can tip for easy entry, and no insider trading. It's
fate, bubby, which technically I believe in, but still, the very mention of it each year seems a little *overt* for those of us deeply rooted
on the earth and making serious plans for next weekend.

I have other concerns. Like many Jewish women my age, I continue to be disturbed about the place of women in Judaism. Once, during early morning prayers at a conservative synagogue to mourn the death of my husband's grandmother, I watched in bleak wonderment as the men, connected to a centuries-old tradition, put on their *tefillin*, wrapping the leather straps around their arms, and headed determinedly (and a tad self-importantly) into their prayer rituals, while the women sat on the sidelines, seemingly irrelevant. "What you were witnessing," whispered one male relative later, "was a Talmudic locker room." It made me glad my daughter was not there to see such male-identified rituals.

I was gladder still to see women taking a much more equal role during services in the reform synagogue we recently joined, despite those misgivings about organized religion. We did so partly because the children, at eight and ten, needed to begin the religious and Hebrew instruction that will eventually lead to a bar and bat mitzvah. But we also joined because we needed a place to go, if only to affirm our cultural connection.

Our children go to a school with relatively few Jewish children, and because most of the friends they have made are not Jewish, I expected them to put up a fuss, to whine and moan about this interruption to their days, and the long drive to the synagogue three times a week. But what really surprised—touched—us was how willing they were to give it a try, and how interested our son was, anyway, in the services we attended together. He did, however, quickly flip through the prayer book and with a none-too-subtle groan, count the All Rises.

It made me realize that children need spiritual information almost as much as they need to learn math. And receiving it doesn't turn them all into raving fundamentalists. It merely makes their lives richer, and the lives of their parents, too.

We went to a family service not too long ago—a Friday night welcome for the new members, which had been preceded in our home by my frantic and humourless attempts, late Friday afternoon, to get both children, tired and unspeakably grubby at week's end, into presentable shape to show up at the synagogue. By the time we got into the car to go, all of us were having nervous breakdowns. (Many modern women will tell you that having the Sabbath begin on a Friday at sundown is a conspiracy against working women.)

It was not until halfway through the service that I felt a calmness that had eluded me all week steal over me. Sitting next to my husband, flipping through the prayer book, half of which is written in English, I came across my favourite line from the service: "Days pass, the years vanish, and we walk sightless among miracles." I spent a while with that line, absorbing it, rolling it around in my head, silently admiring its beauty and its toughness. Minutes later, Martin, not knowing I had been studying it, leaned over and pointed it out to me, whispering that it was his favourite line. Aah. So fate (and God) had Her reasons after all for bringing us together, just so we could sit in temple on a rainy Friday night and be moved by the same line of poetry.

The rate of intermarriage has been rising, and lately, there has been an impassioned and renewed call from every level of Judaism—orthodox through reform—to curb assimilation. More than one Jewish leader has said that intermarriage is as much of a threat to the community as anti-Semitism.

When I hear such statements, I think indignantly that I belong to a community that still, if it had its druthers, wouldn't have me. Other times, I acknowledge I don't do enough as a Jew. My husband's parents are impassioned activists who do good works in three countries, an impossible act for us to follow, even if we were so inclined.

If I believed wholeheartedly in reincarnation, I probably wouldn't have to look further for an explanation of why I feel so comfortable as a Jew. (*Perhaps I have been down this road before.*) But I don't, and so I search for more concrete reasons. Looking back, it seems to me now that I may have, at thirty, benignly confused a religion and a culture and its values with something much more immediate and seductive and important to me: a family. It is not that the religion is unimportant, only that it is a never-ending process of examining, questioning, and yes, arguing. Jews love to argue with God.

When I began to study the rudiments of Judaism, it was, for me, like opening Pandora's box, a box that is still open as my children begin to question me more and more. I am challenged, not only on what I now believe, but on what I used to believe—and have since left behind.

Once, during my latter-day Christian period, when I was wrestling with the question of whether to convert, I consulted a woman whose wisdom I valued. She was irritatingly neutral on the subject. But after I made the decision, after I finally converted, she, who is Jewish, expressed pleasure: "You needed a tribe to belong to," she told me. I did, I do, and I'm grateful.

MESSED-UP MIDDLE AGE

*M*iddle age used to mean fussy-looking matrons in matching sweater sets. Adults drinking highballs and talking about sending their kids off to university. People whose lives (at least to younger people) seemed almost finished, and who certainly did not have any auditory connection to rock and roll, except to yell periodically, "Turn that damn music down!"

However, because of that interesting little demographic trend according to which I and many others had our children late in our reproductive lives (but at the same time refused to admit we were getting any older), middle age now means something entirely different: parents with wrinkled faces and the latest Levis reporting for the pre-school picnic. New mothers in their forties struggling desperately through those jagged crying infant nights. Children pleading with their parents to turn down Bonnie Raitt on the stereo so they can study. Middle age today is all messed up.

I remember feeling sorry for the women I knew who married early and had babies in their twenties. I visited one friend once in her small, dreary apartment and watched her do the laundry, and I thought, "I won't let this happen to me." But who's feeling sorry for whom today? Her kids are probably employed by now. By the time our youngest child is old enough to vote, I may be too old to remember which candidates are running.

Perhaps I exaggerate, but sometimes I wonder if we all thought this through as carefully as we should have. I occasionally run into forty-something women looking energetic and lovely who tell me their children are off to university next year, and I get a little wistful. Had to have that career, didn't you, I tell myself. Had to date for a decade or so. That constitutes a fairly long line of princes who turned into frogs. Had to take my own sweet time.

Well, frankly yes, I did. My work wasn't just something I did. It was a passionate commitment. And as for love, despite all this pop-sociological blarney about *choosing* to stay single and *choosing* to have children late in life, the right man and the right moment did not come together for me until I was in my thirties, so there you are.

Now here I am—forty-something, and still into rock and roll after all these years. My children and I get up in the morning and sometimes we put on Van Morrison singing "Brown-eyed Girl," and we boogie. And I feel ridiculously happy that I'm still listening to this music, and watching my children whirl around the room to it.

But there is sadness there as well. I vowed I would not publicly indulge in my generation's overt *nostalgie de la bod*, joining the women and men who have written regretfully about their fallen body parts. I went to a party recently at which one woman actually turned to someone she didn't know and said, "Do you mind if I ask you a question? I want you to be totally honest. You see that woman across the room? She and I went to school together. Now, tell me, do I really look as old as she does?" When I heard this, I was appalled. Do we really need to do this to ourselves?

But privately, that is another story. On a bad Sunday morning, when the phrase "family life" seems like a contradiction in terms, I browse through old photo albums and come upon a hot picture of my 24-year-old self in red satin tap shorts and a bikini top. For a while, I carry it around with me, showing it to friends—*See, this is what I used to look like, this is who I used to be*. But I put it away after one friend suggested it was shameless of me to whip it out in a restaurant. (The waiter loved it, though.)

Surely, this is an important moment in the aging process, that day you finally realize that you will never again be the woman in the red satin tap shorts. Never mind that the woman in the red satin tap shorts was miserable, however tight her thighs—she was frantically driven, full of self-doubt, and really rather lonely.

In any event, there are other, more searing revelations in store for us in middle age, the most important one perhaps best defined long ago by the American writer Katherine Anne Porter, when she said in an interview: "It is my firm belief that all our lives we are preparing to be somebody or something, even if we don't do it consciously. And the time comes one morning when you wake up and find that you have become irrevocably what you were preparing all this time to be. Lord, that could be a sticky moment . . ."

Porter, who wrote the novel *Ship of Fools*, had no children and travelled all over the world with various lovers, so I guess her idea of sticky moments did not include wiping, for the one-hundredth time, peanut butter off the laminated place mats.

It is clear to me this summer that, despite my relative equanimity, the pleasure I take in my children, my husband, our rich life together, my work, I have aging on my mind. I'm pondering its ultimatums, trivial and profound. Should I go blonder? Drag my family to France for a year? Dare to write a book? On some days, I seem pathetically eager, short of lying or liposuction, to reverse the clock. On others, I feel grateful that I had my children when I did, after all the madness of my twenties was over.

Still, whatever I do, the fact doesn't change: I am slouching toward middle age. And really, the only thing I can think of is that it is way too soon. Which is precisely, I suppose, what those long-ago matrons in their matching sweater sets thought too.

WHEN I'M 64

One evening in early spring, Martin asked me to go with him to an old folks' home—a beautifully decorated and well-run residence in which he and some others had invested. I went reluctantly. I had a million things to do, and besides, I'm not entirely comfortable with the role that requires you to be introduced as Ms. Here-Because-My-Husband-Is.

I walked through the front door somewhat grumpily into a land of chintz (some of it plastic because of, well, accidents), pale walls, artificial flowers, and lined, weathered faces looking eagerly for someone to talk to.

A gentleman in his late eighties attached himself to me. Bill held my hand, flirted with admirable gusto, and asked if I would come and see his room. We slowly made our way along the corridor to a small room packed with gorgeous mahogany furniture. There were family photos everywhere—a younger Bill, with his wife and children; the children with *their* children.

I presumed Bill's wife had died because she was not there with him. But Ellen, he told me, was in worse shape than he was, and required more care. She lived in another home, which was a good half-hour's bus ride from this one. "How often do you see her?" I asked, prepared for answers ranging from "Oh, a couple of times a week" to a vague "Well, it's kind of difficult to get there."

But Bill said he saw his wife every day—because he was the one who fed her her lunch. No matter what the weather, he would get on the bus, travel to his wife's Extendicare home, feed her, and then travel back, where his own lunch, kept warm in the kitchen for him, was waiting. He seemed to think it was only right for him to do this for her, and his only measure of pride was in being physically able to manage it.

I couldn't help flashing forward to our old age—and the twilight years of our entire generation. How many guys do I know now who would make that bus trip every day to feed their wives? Oh sure, I can hear the excuses already, delivered in a quavering voice: "I'm sorry, hon, I'm in denial . . . I just can't handle the fact that you drool . . . I need to play with my drum set . . . I'm allergic to those bus fumes . . ."

Or how many women would do it? The tone of voice gets a little sharper in this fantasy: "I'm much too busy with my Women Who Have Served Too Many Meals support group . . . and according to my calculations, it's *your* turn to do something nice for me . . . I just can't do the dance of dependency any more, darling . . ."

Somehow, it seems dicey. It's not that we are completely self-ish—many of us, after all, are bringing up children and willingly giving them the majority of our time and attention. We also try very hard at our marriages (those who still have them), carefully making sure our spouse has time for himself, but also assiduously addressing our own needs—the first generation of women to do so with the sanction (well, sort of) of society.

But we do seem to have an uneasiness about giving within marriage, as evidenced by the reaction of friends if you tell them you like to, say, bring your spouse coffee in bed occasionally. "What does he do for you?" asked one friend pointedly, as if, without a quid pro quo, you were a sucker.

Well, time marches on, and even people with Nordic tracks and heavily pencilled daytimers grow old (and yes, *yes* we will wear the bottoms of our easy-fit jeans rolled). Time marches on, and if you're lucky enough to stay with someone, or even to find someone new, there will come a day when one of you is in desperate need and the other is not. (There may also come a day when there are no homes, Extendicare or otherwise, to go to, but that is another story.)

As we drove back from the nursing home, the sky was darkening. I took my husband's hand in mine and thanked him for giving grumpy old me the opportunity to have my own little "When I'm 64" epiphany. That relevation went something like this: Take a good look at your partner now, because the day will come when you will have to decide whether you're on the bus or off the bus.

COTTAGE DREAMS,
COTTAGE REALITY

*E*ach summer we go away to visit my husband's parents in the Laurentians. There, in a beautiful log cabin in an exquisite, jewelled northern setting, we experience the multigenerational holiday dream—for about twenty minutes.

The dream is a nice one. The children play happily while their grandparents, and often aunts, uncles, and cousins, spend the kind of time getting to know them that is denied them in their daily life, we being a Montreal–Toronto family. Grandparents ooh and aah appreciatively over all the changes in each child, and paddle about in the water with them. We convene, sun-burned, around the big oak dining-room table for jocular mealtimes. When my husband and I are not with the children, or helping good-naturedly with the chores, we are supposed to be lying around reading good or trashy books, depending on our mental fatigue, or having an intimate moment dockside.

Now, the reality. For some reason, that is the week our kids manifest every neurotic symptom in the book. The younger child won't go outside because the mosquitoes might get her, and then every night she has nightmares; how can the grandparents *sleep* through this? Our older child has decided to be clingy beyond all reason. The children are unspeakably noisy in the early morning, and it's so claustrophobic that our elders can hear every teeth-clenched disciplinary word we fling their way. We, the adult children, are reduced to whining, "but they're not always like this!" in defence of our maladjusted brood.

Meanwhile, my in-laws, only trying to be helpful, intervene with child-rearing tips, often prefaced by that legendary phrase of my mother-in-law's that has, over the years, set off many an alarm bell with all her children: "May I make a suggestion? . . ." None of which I am gracious enough to accept.

Desperate for diversion at the dinner table, I bring up my views on a hot political issue and nearly get lunged at. As for intimacy, don't make me laugh. Every time my husband goes to put his arm around me, either our children need us or I am wanted in the kitchen to peel potatoes or we are not speaking anyway. Plus those walls are so thin.

My husband has developed years of interesting, uh, strategies to cope with this extended togetherness, including breaking world records for time spent in the bathroom and taking suspiciously long berry-picking walks. After any protracted time there, in the magical place where he spent his childhood summers, he somehow turns back into a very large and genial twelve-year-old, waving heartily at me from the dock. Which of course tremendously irritates me. On the other hand, I, too, feel my adult will dissipating to the point where I'm a . . . Stepford daughter-in-law, passively going along with the program, until something jars me, and I wonder, why is it so hard to co-exist with another generation? Do they feel the same way about us?

Of course, all these thoughts seem churlish when the dream returns, as it always does, this time on a golden late afternoon. The sun is glinting off the dock, and the children are having a wonderful time—you can hear them calling to each other in the water. I catch my mother-in-law's eye, and we connect and smile. It is a moment that is both moving—and memorable. Three generations, embracing summer.

And so it goes. At four o'clock, we congratulate ourselves for our excellent choice in parents, in-laws, children, and weather, as if we had anything to do with that kind of luck. By ten o'clock, after a testy dinner during which we ran out of things to talk about, and after which neither of us felt like getting beaten again at Scrabble by my mother-in-law, the kids aren't settling down, the sky is harbouring a suspicion of rain for tomorrow, the book I looked forward to reading has turned out to be a dud, and my husband is snoring loudly on the couch. I give up and go cantankerously to bed, thinking that if I continue to eat the way I have been eating, the phrase "tank suit" will take on a whole new meaning.

A BRIEF SEMANTIC
INTERLUDE

"*D*o you know what a woman finds *really* sexy?" I ask my husband. Finally, I've got his attention. He sits up straighter in his chair, his curiosity admittedly piqued, but ready to run for cover should the conversation take a turn for the worse. Most men would rather undergo a root canal than talk about The Relationship. The fact is, discussing The Relationship is, for them, an emotional root canal with no possibility even of anesthesia.

I take his alert silence as permission to continue. "It's a man who asks questions. And I don't mean 'Huh?' or 'Have you seen my suit jacket?' I mean real, deep questions that indicate a profound inter- est in a woman's life and thoughts and even—gasp—an under- standing of that life and those thoughts."

This—I cannot call it a conversation; perhaps a brief semantic interlude?—occurs more often than I'd like to admit around our house. Whatever it is in me that keeps me doggedly striving for more intimacy and connection and juicy discussions of the whole damn thing, is met and matched by whatever it is in him that keeps him avoiding such discussions while at the same time amiably believing we have a pretty good marriage and we should leave it at that.

I chafe at the former, but am eternally grateful for the latter. My paternal grandparents had a difficult, albeit long-playing marriage, and my own parents are divorced. In some ways, I feel I am reinventing the domestic wheel, even taunting the fates. He, on the other hand, the product of parents who still have a lively, loving marriage, takes such happiness for granted.

For me, today's statistics on divorce are not half as compelling as my own address book. It has become a major monument to the social upheaval of the last two decades, with many of my friends requiring not only multiple changes of address as they separate, divorce, and reconstitute themselves, but entirely different alphabetical listings after they take on new names or reclaim their own. I call one of my friends to ask her how things are going between her and her husband, and she says darkly, "Let's just say I'm keeping a lawyer on retainer."

With this kind of black humour, plus that pencilled-in evidence in my address book, I have no business being complacent about my own marriage, and I am not. Nothing can stop me, on occasion, from taking its pulse. There are days when I think I am secretly living in an updated Doris Day movie, days when I'm sure I've become Doris Day on Acid, and then there are all those other days in between.

Sometimes I yearn for romance and I find that, at least for that week, we've let it slip away. He's got three evening meetings and an overnight trip; I've got a deadline to meet and besides I'm too tired. Every woman I meet is permanently Too Tired.

But romance blooms in unlikely situations. He puts his arm around me while we're watching *The National*, and the moment seems more intimate than a candlelight dinner. (Perhaps it is *the* quintessential Canadian moment—me, my beloved, and . . . Peter Mansbridge.) Or, on a Sunday morning outing that does not descend into the nuclear family meltdown, with its concomitant whining and mutual blame ("I thought you were bringing the box of crackers"), we smile at each other triumphantly. Being joined together in the conspiratorial "us against the dynamics of family life" can even lead to an interesting Sunday afternoon nap, provided the children can be distracted by the right video.

I listen to other tales of romantic gestures—"and then, he whisked me to an empty field where a hot-air balloon was waiting . . ."—and they always seem a bit beside the point. Unless he asked her afterward how the air felt on her face, and whether the sensation of flying stirred something in her soul. I'll settle for corner-store flowers—and a few thoughtful questions.

ERRAND BEHAVIOUR

*W*omen lead such secret lives. I'm not talking black lace merry widows and afternoon trysts, although I'm sure there is enough of that going on somewhere. (Not in my life, I might add.) I'm talking the day-to-day stuff that gets done, mainly by women, despite the fact that some of us hold down difficult jobs or do marathon community work or herculean domestic duty. There is the outward life, the external things we get the credit for (being a brain surgeon *and* president of the PTA for instance), and then there are Errands.

Errands. In my dictionary, an errand is defined as "a short trip to do a thing for someone else." That could also be expanded into a workable definition of motherhood, except the short trip turns into twenty years.

In my former life as a single person, I once joked to a friend that I needed a leave of absence to buy an outfit for a date. What did I know then? Being a wife, mother, and a worker is when you really need the leave of absence. When do the birthday presents get bought, the dry cleaning picked up, or the old shoes taken in for repair?

School is starting up again. Do you know what this means? New shoes, new socks, new underwear, lunch bags, backpacks, booster shots, haircuts. Perhaps my husband will take them for the haircuts, but the clothes shopping remains my turf. Would you trust a man to buy clothing for his children when his last experience in a store was buying a trench coat in four and a half minutes? When he said, "It's great, I'll take it," even the salesman was astonished: "Sir, wouldn't you at least like to look in the mirror?" he asked. No, that kind of slam bam, don't wrap it, I'll wear it approach might miss something crucial, like the fact that our son only likes tight-fitting turtlenecks, or our daughter needs a size smaller than her age depending on the item. Thus it falls to me to wander through stores, as if in a daze, fingering the back-to-school bargains while my work piles up on my desk.

I know I am not alone. There was the editor I know with two children under the age of five, leaving for a complicated three-day business trip one afternoon. Where was she that very morning? On the prowl for white ruffled panties for her toddler to wear to a wedding. Was there no one else who could manage to perform this top-level task? "Not really," she shrugged. "Besides," she added with a little smile, "I wanted to."

Then, pushing the boundaries of rational behaviour, there was the woman who, when asked by a friend to go to lunch, said, "I'd love to but can you walk out with me while I do an errand?" What was the errand? She was buying a bow tie for her *ex-husband* to wear to a formal wedding. (I like to think that if I ever had an ex-husband, the last thing I would be doing on my lunch hour is buying him clothes.)

Clearly, there should be errand analysts, willing to dissect the psychological nuances of errand-running. My own pathology is fairly obvious. I have trouble ceding control of some of these domestic tasks.

However, doing errands is not totally gender specific. I have felt deep pity for men, including my own husband, watching them trudge wearily home from the hardware store on a beautiful Saturday morning, knowing in my heart, as they do not yet, that the household part they are clutching to their chests is not the right size, and that they will be back in the store again, this time flooded with a deep existential angst. Is this what our lives have been reduced to?

If those outside errands are not enough to render us committable, there are household repairs. Finally, repair people are getting wise and scheduling housecalls on weekends and evenings. Otherwise, someone has to stay home during the day, and most people can't. Even when I worked outside at a rented office, it was always I who stayed home. In fairness, my job is more flexible, and my office was close by. But does that mean I deserved to be held hostage by two Maytag deliverymen, as I was one day?

Their visit, to install a new washing machine, resulted in a three-hour opera of dramatic incidents culminating in one of them screaming in pain as he burned his hand on our hot-water pipe, which in turn forced me first to run around with ice cubes and a tube of Polysporin, and then to leap into my car during noon-hour traffic to hunt down a replacement piece of pipe.

When it was all over and I was back at my office, too sweat-soaked and exhausted to even turn on my computer, my husband called to ask me cheerfully how my day was going. Let's just say there was a certain edge in my reply.

No one ever gives you credit for having done errands. No one ever says, "Gee, your child has sneakers that fit this season," or even, "My, you have a working washer and dryer, how clever of you." It is only the guilt that kicks in when we don't do errands, like the time my daughter confessed that the shoes she had kept at school *for six months* did not fit her. And my Bad Mother alert light went on. (What must the teacher think?)

When my children first learned to talk, they always clamoured to come when I said I was going to "do errands." If I ever took them, though, they complained vociferously the whole way. I finally realized they thought I had said I was going to "do Aron."

We have a very engaging family friend by that name, and they could not figure out why he never showed up on these endless rounds. It occurred to me that perhaps I am the only woman left still *doing errands*. Maybe everyone else is *"doing Aron,"* or Joe or Philippe. Which is when the black lace merry widow would come in handy, I guess. But then, I'd have to find the time to go out and shop for it.

MY WHITE NORTH AMERICAN
MALE VALENTINE

*I*s it possible to feel sorry for the white North American man today? Feminism has stripped him of his once-assured dominance in male–female relationships, the economic downturn has robbed him of his good-provider role, and political correctness, and a necessary righting of racial wrongs, has turned his being white— which used to be his toasty warm security blanket—into a defensive posture. On talk shows, in bookstores, where they now sell tomes with titles like *The New Masculinity*, in society in general, he is being urged to come up with a better version of himself.

I think of this occasionally as I watch my husband go through his daily paces. After he's taken out the garbage, fed the kids breakfast, and worked a week of eleven-hour days, fuelled by a combination of sheer economic terror and innate drive, I wonder whether he should be doing . . . gender homework. Getting in touch with his male energy. Going to workshops. Healing his Fisher King wound.

For the most part, the men's movement seems to be something happening apart from him and most men he knows. But I suspect he would relate a little to a comment made by one male activist in *Man Overboard*, a provocative book about men today by Canadian author Ian Brown: "Our lives suck," says one guy. "We're white

North American men, supposedly the envy of the world. Why doesn't it feel good?"

It doesn't feel good because the perks are gone but the responsibilities are not. It doesn't feel good because the economic ante has been upped but the chances of surviving, let alone thriving, have been cut in half. It doesn't feel good because a lot of men are hitting the wall, acknowledging their professional lives have not turned out exactly as they dreamed. And (if men are honest enough to admit it) it doesn't feel good because on top of these pressures, it has become acceptable for women to demand (and receive) at least the semblance of participation in a wide range of domestic chores, from the all-important nurturing of children to more mundane household tasks.

In one of the most dispiriting passages in *Man Overboard*, Brown says that the complaint he heard most often from men was that they shouldered an unfair burden of child-care, especially given their other responsibilities. (This would have most women I know rolling on the floor laughing, except they're already lying on the floor exhausted.) One man actually confessed, "You end up . . . faking it. You hear your wife's car pull up and you turn off the television and throw your kid up in the air." All right, this is indeed infuriating. But on the other hand, let's not forget that women have faked a few things over the years too.

I truly think that men have changed profoundly, and they (and we as women) are still grappling with the results. I see it in my home, I see it in my friends' lives, as men start to grasp the idea— and it is revolutionary—that what happens at home is at least as important as what happens in their work.

I called one man recently to see if his son could play with mine, and, well, I couldn't get him off the phone. His wife was out of town and that morning—wouldn't you know it—the dishwasher had broken down, and this normally quite reticent man, his every molecule tenderized by two weeks alone on the home front with two small children, admitted that he "felt like crying." I didn't exactly say

"Weep, Baby, weep," into the phone, but I did think, ah, he's beginning to sniff the sheer loneliness that most men manage to miss, and most women, once their kids are older, recall with a shudder. Another man, a friend I like a lot, stood in my kitchen having a drink one night and said, with very little prompting, "Marriage is the hardest thing I've ever done." I wasn't as struck by the complaint as I was by his commitment. He was in there, he was working at it. It wasn't just something he came home to.

I see how connected my husband is to the children, not just on a macro aren't-they-something basis but on a more visceral level in their daily lives—lives which once a day yield momentous, shaping events for them.

And I see how connected he is to me. Despite all my black humour about his intimacy capacity, when he calls me from out of town, or even just from the office, I often experience a Houston-to-spacecraft sensation. I see that what we have is a work-in-progress. It is punctuated with frustration on both sides but cemented by this idea, and ideal, of being loving, equal, and intimate partners, both of us struggling to do our bit for the family and chase the dragon's tail of personal fulfillment.

Sometimes I worry, having gotten what I want—a writing life, a family—whether I've done it at his expense. Have I punctured his dreams? (I don't think he worries in the same way about me, frankly.) And I think women who have worked so hard to liberate themselves are now going to have to deal with the legitimate anger so many men feel about the extreme corners into which they have been painted—either villified as brutish predators or made into docile house pets.

All of which is to say I think it is as hard today to be a man as it is to be a woman. But try finding that message on a Valentine's card.

THAT TROLL ON THE TABLE

For weeks now, there has been a troll on the breakfast table. He has blue hair, he is bare-chested, and his short black pants don't quite cover his cute little backside. Sometimes he is lounging in the fruit bowl, other times he's propped up against it. Every time my eyes come into contact with him I want to whimper, for that troll is a symbol of our heroic struggle to control the ever increasing mountain of junk in our lives.

I call this junk UPOs—unidentified plastic objects—and I curse the manufacturers, promoters, and distributors of it, even as I ask myself what it is doing in my home. I could understand the mess when the children were tiny. Those were the days when, after they were asleep, I would lie comatose on our bed and hear my husband come in, and it would sound as if he had a peg leg as he made his way across the floor, picking up tow trucks, blocks, and large Raggedy Anns as he went. But why is it, with two children who are no longer Fisher-Price's best customers, who are nine and seven for God's sakes, that our house still seems littered with *stuff*?

What stuff, you ask? Well, over here, in the same breakfast area that has been seized by the troll, on a shelf that is supposed to be limited to art supplies, stand two Goofy statues, no doubt picked up from a McDonald's (what, it isn't enough they have bad food that kids adore, they have to hand out stupid plastic statues as well?). One Goofy has a pipe cleaner wound around his nose, the other, a piece of black electrical tape over his mouth. Clearly, one of my children has made a creative statement. Or how about this upper half of a Barbie? I am not capable, on any level, of dealing with Barbie's breasts first thing in the morning.

Then there is that bag of plastic eyeballs, which I concede is important: our daughter is a serious artist who, in between her bowl of puffed wheat and getting her shoes tied for school, will whip up an amazing mixed-media collage. Although the puffed wheat element of it does tend to deteriorate over time.

Apart from the UPOs, there is other detritus, like this box of Dr. Ballard's dry food for puppies, which my husband picked up at a promotion seven months ago during a walk through a mall. We don't actually have a dog, but of course we might get a dog, and in the meantime, it has become part of our permanent collection, joining the rest of the crowd: old keys—to what, I haven't a clue; stray pieces of paper with obscure phone numbers; school bulletins (I've read them but has he?); math homework (whose? due when?); coupons for pedicures; instructions on de-lousing your kids (*never* throw them out); paper clips, elastic bands from the morning newspaper, old pencil sharpeners, and old pencils; ponytail holders; and pennies as far as the eye can see.

And what about this note on a faded piece of red construction paper, in shaky printing: "Mom I love you, you are the greatest." I am incapable of throwing out any love notes from my children. There is a practical side to my sentimentality. What if I need evidence during the teen years that they didn't always find me pathetic? Perhaps I should laminate them. (The notes, not the children.)

Part of the mess stems from the fact that we have chosen to make our breakfast nook a central creative area. And so we have held numerous family meetings about it during which we drill home the message *pick it up and put it away*. We have bought baskets and labelled them hopefully—pencils go *here*, glue and string go *there*. We have invested in a kitchen filing system and put the names of each family member on a file. We have put up a very spiffy store-bought "no flyers" notice at the front door, which has cut down on the 2-4-1 pizza coupons that would otherwise be sitting untouched on the counter. And each week, it seems, we throw or give away bags of stuff.

When we visit other households, I am on the lookout for their junk as avidly as a police drug dog sniffing a suitcase, keeping my eyes peeled for special trap doors through which they throw their stray Barbie torsos. (I once discovered a basement in the home of one of my most meticulous friends that was truly gothic in its crazed collection of junk.) In fact, my eyes narrow when I see a perfectly put-together kitchen with nothing in it but, say, kitchen implements. How *anal*, I think, gritting my teeth.

I have a deep-seated suspicion that my desperate attempts to order this stuff neatly are not simply a household issue for me. They are a sanity isssue, a way to say, Yes! I can fashion order out of this chaos called family life.

And so I keep trying, while that troll on the table laughs and laughs.

BACK TO SCHOOL BLUES

*B*ack to school was simple when I was a child. You got a new pencil case, maybe some new shoes, and you went off on that first day with butterflies in your stomach, hoping your new teacher was not a complete ogre. As for our parents, they just packed us off, relieved that a steady routine was at hand.

Perhaps for our children the ritual remains the same, but for the parents, the routine is utterly different—and more than a bit disturbing. We pack them off all right, but in between finding the pencil cases and new shoes, we are on the phone to each other, planning strategy, scheduling important meetings, alert and ready for what looks like battle.

How did it come to this? The public school system, as just about everyone agrees by now, is under siege. Today's parents have risen up, all of a sudden appalled that their Mackenzies and Taras, their Joshuas and Daniels, cannot by Grade 5 write a sentence without spelling errors.

Everyone has a favourite horror story, but my latest one is this: a parent I know goes in to complain to her principal that her son, in Grade 3, cannot add or subtract, multiply or divide. "Have you tried teaching him with popsicle sticks?" the principal asks. This same parent is now paying $20,000 a year, and putting her family through the financial mill, to send her children to a private school.

And so we are confused and angry, frustrated too, by the incomprehensible jargon the educators use to explain or, in more cases, defend themselves. *They* use words like "benchmarks" and "futures ed" and "holistic marking." *We* use words like "grammar" and "spelling" and "standards." They talk about "learning outcomes." We talk about pass or fail. This debate reminds me of a line from a Margaret Atwood poem: it is "a duet with two deaf singers."

At one meeting, we are told, "There are no external standards by which your children are being judged," an admission that causes a tableful of parents to become apoplectic. One of us asks, "Every day, as adults, we go out into the world and we are evaluated professionally. Are you telling us our children should not have to suffer the real consequences of mastering or not mastering their work?"

The response confuses us further, but when the parents in my "study" group—two lawyers, a doctor, and me—indicate we cannot understand the new system, we are told not to worry. It took the educator—a bright, dedicated teacher who worries about her own children in the system—a year or so to get it as well! Welcome to the Orwellian world of modern education.

Back home, I recognize there is an irrationality to my rage: my children, so far, are flourishing. Admittedly still in the early grades, they are in a progressive inner-city school where the principal looks like someone my mother might not have let me date. He wears an earring in one ear, a lot of black tee-shirts, and black jeans. He also happens to be an extraordinary principal, running an inspired school.

How can you fault a school in which the children get sent to the principal's office not only when they've done wrong, but when they've done right? When my son mastered a particularly difficult French story, he was sent down to read it to the principal. And he will never forget it.

How can you fault a school that has reduced the number of playground incidents and made learning more stress-free by teaching children how to deal peaceably with their conflicts? A school that, under board policy, has made repeated racist remarks an expulsion offence? On the other hand, new and improved social values do not replace concrete knowledge: this same principal must convince a lot of doubting parents that their children are learning the three Rs as well. So far, I find I'm on his side more often than I'm not.

Last spring, he allowed himself to be the main draw in a funfair game, standing good-naturedly while the kids threw wet sponges at his head to get a prize. Watching him, I thought, this is probably easy compared to what the parents throw at him.

And what is the prize *we* are after for our children? The glow of real achievement, the pain of stretching their brains to accommodate this thing called knowledge. I want my children to have what we had (a sound education in grammar, reading, mathematics, and other subjects) but I want them to apply these skills in a world that even I have trouble coping with—hungrily competitive, overloaded with information, and filled with domestic and global stress.

I also want, on a personal basis, to come away from just one school meeting this year feeling I've understood what I've been told. I want this debate over education to stop being a duet with two deaf singers.

RACISM, HEART AND SOUL

*O*ne afternoon, our six-year-old son came home with a form for me to sign. "Mom, I need to take this back tomorrow. Sign it please." I stared at it, gathering my thoughts. This took more than a moment. "Honey, this is an application for you to join a Black Heritage class after school." He nodded. "Well," I started slowly, "you are already enrolled in a Hebrew Heritage program, and that might be enough for Grade 1. And besides, uh, you're not black."

He was mortally offended. What did being black have to do with it? One of his best friends was going to take Black Heritage, a pal with whom he had spent a previous year in Hebrew Heritage, and he's not black, so there! Couldn't he *please* take Black Heritage? Please?

I stuck with my refusal on the legitimate grounds that one after-school program was enough this year, and that we were already committed to Hebrew Heritage, but deep down, I actually felt it was a little weird for a white child to take a Black Heritage class. That immediately sparked a doubt in me as I asked myself if I had wandered into the swampy territory of racism. Like those motion-sensitive security lights that flicker on at the hint of movement nearby, we are all hyperconscious of the issue of racism these days. But how are we doing with the reality? You can learn a lot by checking in with the children.

While Jonathan was arguing with me about his right to go to Black Heritage, his close friend—let's call him Zack—who was already enrolled in it, was having his own racial epiphany. Zack has a Jewish mother and a father of mixed heritage from Jamaica. Zack's mother thought her child understood where he was from and what he was all about until the day she heard him and a group of friends taunting an East Indian boy out on the sidewalk, yelling, "Darky, darky, darky." In a flash, she had hauled Zack inside the house and given him a crucial lecture: "One-quarter of your relatives are black! This is a part of who you are. You don't go making fun of the colour of people's skin!"

Zack held his pale-skinned hand up to the light. "Mom, I just don't see it," he said, "where's the black?" Frustrated, his mother replied, "Honey, in your *heart*, you're black, in your *soul* you're black."

So Zack enrolled in Black Heritage, and my son stuck with Hebrew for this year, and I began to get a sense of how diligently some schools today deal with racial attitudes: most of the students in the Black Heritage program were, indeed, white, and they were learning more than their parents will ever know about black culture. (Some kids swore it was the coolest after-school program going.)

Back when I went to school, the classrooms were boringly homogeneous, and there was hardly an acknowledgment of anything outside the white Christian norm. Our attitudes—whether tolerant or wildly bigoted—were shaped in the home, and never challenged outside of it.

But in my children's downtown Toronto school, racial and cultural and religious differences are celebrated. (You haven't experienced true multiculturalism until you've heard a student say Happy Holidays in Urdu, as one did at a recent pageant.) Sometimes these efforts are taken to absurd and almost satirical heights—holiday pageants that fail to mention Christmas are one contemporary idiocy, along with banning Christmas carols, the traditional, beautiful ones that carry a hint of spirituality, and replacing them with "value-free" songs like "Frosty the Snowman." (There is too a value being inculcated by singing "Frosty"—it's called mediocrity.)

At our school, there is a large Asian student population (almost half of my daughter's kindergarten class is Oriental). And many of those Asian parents who speak little or no English have, rather bravely I think, put their children into French Immersion. A sign is posted on the glass window of the office in this French/English school: *Ici, le racisme n'a pas sa place.* Any schoolyard racial incident is resolved in the principal's office, with stern warnings given to the perpetrators. There are not all that many repeat offenders.

If you operate on the premise that racism is learned and not inherent, then we should automatically be turning out children who will become more tolerant adults. Of course, we won't know for years to come whether this hands-on approach to racism really works. On the days when my son comes home chanting some pidgin rhyme poking fun at the Chinese, I think we are all being naive and idealistic. On the days when I wonder uneasily why it is my children, in the heart of a multicultural city, have so few friends with skins of different colour, I think we are all turning a blind eye to a reality that persists and persists, despite any and all efforts to change it.

But then there are those other days, when I am forced to see things a little differently, when a child leads the way, when my son fervently believes, in his heart and soul, that a Black Heritage program exists for him, as well as for anybody else. Those are the days when I think we are all changing for the better.

SEX IN THE NINETIES:
VICTIMS AND MONSTERS

I read the news today, oh boy. And what a disturbing read it was. Before I had even had my coffee, and as my children were loudly enjoying their Cheerios, there leapt out at me, on page one of my morning paper, the story of an incest trial in which the father, who repeatedly assaulted his daughter from the age of five onwards, said he had wanted to be the first to break her in. In this story, sex equalled victim and abuser and a childhood lost forever, despite a jail term and a hefty settlement.

I got to the office, began on page one of another newspaper, and encountered in one section the following stories:

- "Immigration officials launch sex harassment investigation": a woman was defying a deportation order after claiming she had rebuffed the sexual advances of an immigration officer. Sex equals victim and harasser.
- "MD loses licence after sex assaults": a doctor, who admitted to masturbating between seeing patients, had fondled and assaulted patients on home visits. Sex equals an abusive power relationsip and a horrible breach of trust.
- "Sexual abuse a guilty secret in sports": sex equals coercion, and claims victims even among physically fit female achievers.

The previous night, I had watched a television documentary that told the story of a controversial murder case and the sexually violent slaying of a nine-year-old girl, whose brother had admitted to having had sex with her. In one shot, the cameras panned over the covers of certain child porn mags belonging to one suspect, including one called *Deeper, Daddy, Deeper.* And the night before *that*, I had seen another news documentary about a man who had raped four of his daughters. He is now in jail, while they, as adults, continue to suffer. Sex equals pain and trauma for the rest of one's life.

If I were a teenage girl absorbing these stories, wondering how to begin actively exploring my own sexuality, I think I might be fearful and depressed. I would wonder whether the world out there was really like this, cruel and dangerous, ripe with the possibility that anyone can violate your trust—an immigration officer, a doctor, a father. If I were a teenage boy, I think I might feel guilty and confused. I would wonder whether I was the type to do these horrible things, and even if I wasn't, whether I would be blamed for them anyway. And if I were a seven-and-a-half-year-old, having learned to read, and having decided to scan the newspaper for the s-e-x word, I think I would grab my teddy bear and head for neverland.

Instead I am a grown-up, and a mother, trying hard here not to sound like the kind of prude who wants to ban rock and roll lyrics. (Hey, I'd like to write them.) But I will admit to feeling my heart grow heavy as I absorb this daily smorgasbord of sexual aberration. In some curious way, it has become its own form of assault—this sexual harassment/abuse/deviance reportage, in which we have gone, in a very short while, from pretending incest never happens to asserting it happens almost all the time, from denying the existence of any sexual harassment to creating a whole genre of victims and victim-speak and quasi-judicial hearings to sort it all out.

In the media, sex in the nineties seems to equal harassment, abuse, assault, and breach of trust. Victims and monsters. Or if we lighten up on abuse, we send that other sombre message—sex in the nineties can be terminal.

Yes, you can get AIDS from doing it, but reading about it can lay you low too, resulting in a kind of psychological numbness, a reaction to the sheer volume of the disasters of human sexuality.

In this, the age of Oprah, all has been confessed, nothing has been forgiven, and much is being set to rights. I know that I, as the grown-up, have to be clear and positive and helpful in order to raise sexually healthy kids. I know, too, that it is ultimately a good thing that the blinding light of the media is shining at last on all forms of sexual abuse. But sometimes, in the face of all that it requires of me, I long to grab my own teddy bear and head for the hills.

IF YOU BELIEVE IN CHILDHOOD, CLAP YOUR HANDS

*F*or me, the seminal moment in understanding just how sophisticated young children are today came several years ago during a show-and-tell session in a Grade 1 classroom. I had been invited because it was my son's turn. But a little girl in the front row determinedly shot up her hand with a question for *me*: "Is the perfume you're wearing Fendi?" she asked.

I was astonished, not just because I actually was wearing this perfume (God, how much had I put on?), but because I could not believe a six-year-old child would recognize it by name. When I found out later that this child's favourite movie was *Breakfast at Tiffany's*, I was somehow not surprised.

I thought about this recently when I read *The Disappearance of Childhood*, a provocative book written by American cultural critic Neil Postman, published in 1982, and reissued by Vintage/Random House recently with a new preface. In it, Postman argues that we are taking childhood away from our children: "Everywhere one looks it may be seen that the behaviour, language, attitudes and desires, even the physical appearance of adults and children are becoming increasingly indistinguishable," he writes.

He blames the indiscriminate watching of television for this disappearance of childhood. The concept of childhood can only exist,

he tells us, if we foster a separate culture in which children are protected from the often grisly, forceful, violent passions of adulthood,
a culture in which there is a hierarchy of information, one in which
children are slowly initiated into the adult world, its responsibilities
and revelations.

Yet, as anyone who has ever channel-surfed the talk shows can
attest, Oprah, Sally Jesse Raphael, and Geraldo have pried open
whatever closet doors were still shut. There are virtually no adult
secrets left in our society. Any child with the ability to press a button (which most two-year-olds are able to do) can listen in on a discussion about people who have sex with their children, watch a
rape/murder re-enactment on a crime show, or even just troll
through the newscasts to receive an often terrifying vision of how
the world works.

Moreover, millions of small children are hostage to the flickering
screen, which stays on in their homes for hours on end and feeds
them a steady diet of factoids and infotainment that ends up blurring
all the lines—the line between past and present, the line between
shows and commercials, the line between adult and child—making
everyone buyers and sellers alike in the same cultural marketplace.

The result is often incongruous enough to be amusing until one
considers its ramifications: a pre-pubescent sprite I know shimmies
professionally in her kitchen doing an eerie imitation of Marilyn
Monroe purring "Happy Birthday Mr. President." She saw it on
Wayne's World, and each time she does it, her mother winces.
Perhaps the mother senses that as children become more like adults,
the constraints that keep most, if not all, adults in place are loos-
ened, and children become more vulnerable to abuse of all kinds.

It is a very bleak image, this expulsion of children from "the gar-
den of childhood," as Postman describes it. But despite his confi-
dent assertion that his thesis, advanced a dozen years ago, pans out
in every aspect, much has changed since then. He predicted the
demise of Disney, when in fact Disney profits are soaring as children
flock to see quality productions like *The Lion King.*

Moreover, it is no longer just the so-called moral majority that is demanding and winning the right to have viewing codes and standards applied to television material. Many parents who consider themselves both liberal and anti-censorship are changing their minds about what is acceptable in this culture for their children. They are even taking individual action that a few years ago would have seemed to them extreme or prudish.

To my own astonishment, I attached an angry note to a video I was returning to the children's section of one store, complaining about its trashy content, although it occurred to me later I was railing less against the language—a dreary and unimaginative procession of low-level four-letter words—than against a kind of rock-hard cynicism about life and human nature in it that I found appalling.

No one who has ever read a fairy tale or studied history can claim that childhood has ever been carefree. But it need not be laden down, as it is today, with quite so much extraneous knowledge, whether it is a grasp of designer perfumes before you can parse a sentence, a working knowledge of the Paul Bernardo murder trial, or the very real fear that some robbers could burst through the door and get us just as they did on *Rescue 911*: "They did, Mom, I saw them!"

It's time to rescue childhood.

WHO IS THE FAG WHO
KILLED ROCK HUDSON?

*A*t our school's daycare centre, several children were playing Scrabble. One of them triumphantly spelled the word s-e-x. "Ooh," squealed one child, "that will get you a baby." "No," said another more seriously, "that will get you AIDS."

This little epiphany made the daycare instructor sigh. How sad, she said to me when I came to pick up the kids, that the first sexual connection a young child made was between sex and a fatal disease.

We are all sighing a bit these days. We were going to be the generation to raise our children to be sexually healthy. Unrepressed? You bet. Able to get information when they needed it? Of course. None of this hellfire and damnation approach. We were going to *celebrate* sex.

Then came AIDS to alter the sexual landscape, and ever since it began its relentless march through our communities, we have all been grappling with how to inform and protect our children, and more importantly, how to get them to protect themselves.

But the irony is obvious. At the same time as they are learning about sex, they are also having to deal with the knowledge of a deadly disease that goes along with it. Could a fundamentalist conservative anti-sex movement have dreamt up anything more chilling?

Today, our children need to be told there is no such thing as safe sex. There is unsafe sex, and there is safer sex. Today our children, as they become sexually active, will need to know how to ask a sexual partner to use protection. They will need the actual *words*. According to the Toronto Department of Public Health, in the heterosexual community, young girls are becoming increasingly vulnerable to AIDS. You see the urgency here.

My children are young, I am new at this, and I have been surprised already by some of the questions they have asked about sex. Moreover, their access to mass media has given today's kids a rather eccentric sexual education, a surface sophistication that is both funny and painful. One of my children asked me casually in the car if I had AIDS, in approximately the same tone of voice that would be used to inquire whether I had remembered to get Shreddies.

A boy I know was worried about a rash. He shyly showed the affected area to his mother, and then looked relieved when she said it was something minor. "I thought it was a Bobbitt kind of a situation," he explained.

A Toronto sexual health education community worker told me that when she began talking about AIDS in schools several years ago, the first question came from a child who asked, "Who was the fag who killed Rock Hudson?"

How do you even begin to deal with that? She did by talking about names that hurt people, about the origin of the word "fag," about homophobia, about two people mutually agreeing to a sexual act, and about AIDS itself. But you cannot adequately discuss AIDS, she told me, if you have not already done the groundwork—talking to your children when they are very young about the things that make their bodies feel good, about babies, about sexual behaviour.

I am relieved that there are community workers who go into our schools and help lead our children into self-awareness and self-protection. I feel lucky that we live in a social climate in which this isn't seen as gross interference by the state. We need this interference. Without it, it would all be up to us, and some of us, it seems, are simply not up to the task.

These community educators tell me that young teenagers, desperate for information, still want it to come from their parents, and they complain that their parents tell them nothing. Yet many parents tell me their kids do not want to hear what they have to say: "Oh, I gave him a book about it, she's too embarrassed to talk to me directly, he's so naive I don't think he's even interested, she runs screaming from the room."

Sometimes, in our house, I feel we've already failed monumentally: I forgot to mention the joyful aspect of sex . . . and should we tell them masturbation is okay or will they figure that out?

Moreover, there is never a convenient teaching moment. The sex questions in our house usually come when I am rushing in to throw dinner on the table so that one of us can get to another activity. Recently, after my son asked me such a question, I felt like a cross between a slimy politician and a glib talk show host—"I'm glad you asked me that," I panted as I threw down the grocery bags. "Can you save up that question until our next quiet time?" I said, adding emphatically, "I would *love* to answer it."

Luckily, I have determined children. (I'm usually the one who runs screaming from the room.) That question was faithfully brought up at bedtime. The look of gratitude in his eyes as I made myself comfortable on his bedroom floor and launched into a discussion moved me almost to tears. As did his heartfelt "Thanks, Mom" as, later, I left the room.

JUST THE FAX, MA'AM

*M*otherhood is a series of obsessions. When our first child was born, I went through a lifetime of worries all in the first week—he was too quiet, he cried too much, what was the bump on his head? Should we call the hospital about his breathing? He couldn't possibly be getting enough to eat . . . Shh, what's that noise? . . . What is amazing to me now is not that we have two children who are apparently flourishing in their middle childhood years, but that I wasn't committed to an institution along the way.

There is still time. I have now discovered that the opportunities for deeply anxious parental behaviour only expand once your children enter the school system. You can literally go crazy with worry, not only about their actual education, but about all the social and psychological dramas that involve them along the way.

I think every mature parent (and here I'm giving myself the benefit of the doubt) can accept the fact that her kids won't get invited to all the parties, they won't make all the sports teams, their cursive handwriting will be bad enough to get Needs Improving on their report cards, and their teachers won't uniformly think they are God's gift to the school system. But, oh, the passion that wells up when your child is treated unfairly! It evokes something primal in you

("She said *what* about your science project?") as you not only empathize, but relive the psychic bruises you yourself sustained in childhood.

I'll never forget the time that teacher in elementary school sneered at and then rejected my self-portrait, just because I made myself look like Sandra Dee. I was crushed! Today, that teacher would be toast— likely to be hauled over the coals by some alert-for-grievances parent, who would have no difficulty charging her with violating the holy grail of self-esteem. (If my kid thinks she looks like Sandra Dee, that is her right . . .)

Like no other generation before them, the parents of today are advocates for their kids. I see these parents—mainly mothers, because they still seem to be the parents with the most flexible time, but fathers, too—phoning, writing, or showing up at school to help their child deal with a difficult situation, or even just to help their child succeed. When it comes to taking on the system, they have no timidity—and considerable chutzpah.

They do it, damnit, because they care. But do they care too much? Some parents seem to move alarmingly fast to right a wrong, not trusting, for one minute, that the situation could conceivably take care of itself. And when a mother I know recently told me that during one incident involving her son in class, she had actually cried in the principal's office, I thought, I'll never do *that*. No, when my turn came, I did it over the phone, so that my quiet sobbing could be mistaken for a bad allergy.

This was after one of my children had an ego-demolishing encounter with a teacher, who (and here I reluctantly give the teacher the benefit of the doubt) was probably operating out of the best intentions. Teachers are pushed to the wall, and sometimes they just have had it, with a kid, with a circumstance, with the whole system. But teachers can also make very flawed decisions. It is at times like this, when your child comes home sobbing with the news of a great injustice, that you need to take measured action (after, of course, you've called your husband, your mother, and a close friend, and then run maniacally around the house yelling, "I'll rip her throat out").

This is where modern inventions like the fax machine can come in handy. I found myself lavishing more care on the one (or was it two?) fax I sent in outrage (after trying to get through on the phone) than I had on my real work, carefully editing out "appalling," and "unjust," but keeping in "disheartening." Two days this took.

The issue was finally resolved at the principal's level, with the principal not only affirming that our child had been unnecessarily hurt and taking steps to correct it, but gently reassuring me that being what I called "a passionate advocate" for your child is a good thing.

Still, I wondered whether I had gone too far. Every parent knows in her or his heart that it is psychologically healthier for the whole family if children solve most of these problems themselves. The trick, I guess, is in the balance—in knowing how much to care and how far to go; in letting your child (and the school) know you stand behind her, but also allowing her to negotiate her own way through inevitable pitfalls.

Which brings me to the Texas cheerleader murder case, in which the mother was charged with conspiracy to commit murder after she tried to have the mother of her daughter's chief rival for cheerleader blown away. Talk about putting the "hood" back in motherhood. Now there was a mother who didn't run around the house long enough before she took measured action.

By the way, I never did look like Sandra Dee.

H IS FOR HOMEWORK HYSTERIA

*A*t the beginning of the academic year, our school held a curriculum night. In my daughter's Grade 1/2 classroom, the parents were like hungry lions waiting to be fed a piece of meat—which, in this case, happened to be the two teachers who were responsible for the daily care and education of thirty-five lively and diverse six- and seven-year-olds.

As the teachers' eyes widened in dismay, the parents embarked on a rampage: "Why isn't there homework? Why isn't there *more* homework? Why don't you send home math problems for Cassandra?" The nadir of the evening, in my opinion, was reached when one father actually suggested he'd like to have a working supper with his six-year-old son—why, he could do addition and subtraction at the dinner table.

These were little children we were talking about here. Moreover, they were children in a French immersion class. That meant, as the teachers tried to explain, that for the Grade 1s, it would be the first time, in an all-day situation, that they would have to cope with being spoken to, and expressing themselves, completely in another language. This alone is incredibly hard work. But some parents were not buying it. "Homework!" they growled. "Homework!" they pouted. "Homework!" they insisted.

I was appalled. Even back in the good old days, when schools knew how to teach children by gosh, I did not have homework until at least Grade 4. Still, I came away with a superb grounding in grammar and English composition (Thank you, Mrs. Aberle. Thank you, Miss Torrey).

But these parents seemed, well, *driven*. It struck me later that their panic was really more connected to the larger undercurrent of fear and failure running through our whole society today than it was to their immediate concern. Many parents are not making it economically, we are fearful of the future, and so we are going to make damn well sure our children get it right—even if it means taking away their childhood in the process. Even if it means berating a teacher. (It did not surprise me to learn that both teachers wept afterward.)

This is not to detract at all from the legitimate criticisms we have about the educational system, and our need to improve it. Nor does it negate the importance of homework in the later grades. But let's get a grip here. Translating this anxiety into a demand for homework in the primary grades is both ridiculous and anti-child. Besides, at least in our system, there already is homework in the primary grades—a borrow-a-book program in which the child is encouraged to read a story with the parent every night, after which the child's impressions or reading progress are recorded in a little book.

This program cleverly fosters both intimacy and reading skills. And I've found that once we get through that, my daughter is content to snuggle, watch a favourite program, draw pictures, or play with her stuffed animals.

The irony of this homework hysteria is that in the later grades, there is homework all right, and sometimes the parents are up all night doing it. At a recent dinner party I attended, two parents complained about the difficulty of the homework their children had been given. One, a newspaper editor, told how his son in Grade 5 had come home with a request to list, among other things, the names of the lieutenant-governors of all ten provinces. Thank God

Daddy had access to InfoGlobe, but what did the other parents do?

How absurd. On the one hand you've got these parents clamouring for homework when their kids are barely learning the ropes, and on the other, you've got them complaining about having to do it for their children in Grades 4 and 5. And how about a third absurdity—a teacher I know recently took his child to a high-school open house at which another parent actually asked a Grade 9 teacher, "When do you teach the kids to turn the TV off while they do their homework?" In other words, the parent did not consider it his responsiblity to, shall we say, encourage the child toward good study habits.

You want to have a working supper with your six-year-old? Listen to the story of her day over dinner, then take her by the hand after dinner, walk her outside, and show her the night sky. Look at the stars, talk a bit about the constellations, and finally come back in and have a nice cup of hot chocolate together before you tuck her into bed.

That is the child who will be more open and ready to learn what she needs to know, rather than the one whose parents obsess about math problems in Grade 1. Parents, first heal yourselves.

OF CIVILITY I SING

I once knew a woman who confessed to me that when her husband left for work in the morning, if she was angry enough at him, she would open the door and call after him, "I hope you get hit by a truck today!"

I was not married at the time, so I did not quite understand the level of passion and feeling that can rear its head in a long-term relationship. Instead, I wondered: what did her husband shout back? What if the kids heard her? What if he really did die that morning? And finally, did she know someone who could do the job?

After twelve years of marriage, though, I realize that there are days when all that is standing between me and marital disaster is basic civility. In our house, we strive mightily for this civility, and we often fail spectacularly. I am not talking here about a "Good morning, my sweet, aren't the roses lovely?" forced kind of chirpiness you see only in British domestic dramas. We run a pathologically unrepressed household that often takes visitors aback: two passionate and loud people (verging on four, now that the children are six and eight) who, at any given moment, might be arguing—make that discussing with great vehemence—anything from the prospects for peace in the Middle East to whose turn it is at the computer to the sheer idiocy of THE PERSON WHO LEFT THE OVEN ON ALL NIGHT LONG

WHEN IT WAS CLEARLY HIS (or, highly unlikely, HER) RESPONSIBILITY TO TURN IT OFF. Exchanges like the following, I'm sad to say, are not uncommon in our household: "You took my pen." "No I didn't." "Yes you did." "No I didn't." "Yes you did, you always do. . . ." And this is only the adults I'm talking about here.

As our children become older and wiser and able to stand around observing and judging (not to mention copying) us in all our splendid frailty, we have tried to set limits to the level of insult. You can tell someone that was a ridiculous thing to do, for instance, but you can't call your spouse a hopeless jerk, unless you want your child's teacher to hear him or her described that way by your daughter after a particularly lively morning.

We have also tried to institute tone-of-voice checks, as in "Watch your tone" when you realize you are sounding a little like Margaret Thatcher just pointing out to your mate where he might have left his car keys as the children wait impatiently at the back door, or when your spouse takes on that Robert de Niro ("Are you talkin' to me?") menace when you just happen to mention for the fifth time that you're tired of cleaning the breakfast dishes yourself.

Oh, but it is tough. We live immersed in a pop culture that has enshrined domestic rudeness, where every sitcom character's idea of affection is to growl "Get a life, bone-head," where both adults and children sound as if they just passed Sarcasm 101.

I used to dislike the television show *Roseanne* for this reason—wincing as she mercilessly cut down her kids—but I confess she grew on all of us, because the good thing about Roseanne and her show is that it depicts a real live family having a not-so-Leave-It-to-Beaver day. It also portrays a healthy marriage—there is a whole lot of love and lust between Roseanne and her TV husband Dan, in a relationship that feels pretty equal to me. It may be earthy and even crass, but it doesn't have that slimy contempt for each other masquerading as humour. It also does not demean one specific character—there is across-the-board humiliation and triumph for the whole family. And besides, I laugh at the zingers.

However, unless your family is involved in a twenty-two-episode series with an option to renew, it's still inadvisable to try to pull off such brute sarcasm at home, especially when directed toward your kids. You can be funny and gently mocking, but you can't use your wit to strip their gears. (If you do, your kids may grow up to write novels about it after you've paid for their therapy.)

I suppose it's the same with your husband, although it means giving up a lot of really great lines. One solution could be to aim for that light but witty sparring style reminiscent of drawing-room comedy, but is this technically possible without a drawing room?

Still, there are times when you are so at odds with your partner that the words "Have a good day," hurled out of the side of your mouth, sound like a death threat. Which brings up an interesting point: why stoop to actually yelling unpleasantries when civilities, cleverly uttered, can do the job nicely and keep you on the moral high ground?

Have a good day, *darling.*

THIS CRAMP'S FOR YOU

*W*e've all read the greeting card and snickered at the punch line: "What's the difference between a terrorist and a woman with PMS?" Answer: "You can negotiate with a terrorist." It is sort of funny, except on one of those four or five (or is it fifteen?) days of the month when *you're* the woman with PMS, and one of your children is playing, at a criminal decibel level, the soundtrack from *Sister Act 2* ("Get up offa that thing, and dance till you feel better . . ."). Meanwhile the other child is whining "I'm hunnngry" in a voice that is so excruciating to the human ear that remedial surgery may be necessary, and your husband walks in with this vague, "How did I get here" expression on his face. Is he sympathetic, or more to the point, helpful? Nooo. He simply fans through the mail and then goes off upstairs to spend twenty-five minutes looking for his sweatpants as you s-l-o-w-l-y metamorphose into something very ugly in the kitchen. Instead of make my dinner, it's make my day.

If you are squeamish about these things, if the word mini-pad embarrasses you when it is said aloud, if you think even admitting there is a PMS problem is playing into anti-feminist hands, then this is not for you. But for the rest of us, it's time for a PMS powwow.

Here are my personal thoughts: a lot of women I know, especially those in their late thirties and early forties, many of whom have young children, are experiencing more and more physical discomfort and emotional distress around the time of their periods. They deal with it by limiting (sort of) their caffeine intake, drinking lots of water, taking everything from Primrose oil to Prozac, and sincerely attempting to avoid manslaughter charges.

But the emotional fallout is hard to fix. It's difficult even to talk about. Do we tell our children about PMS and then run the risk of having them attribute every behavioural tic, or worse, every perfectly reasonable demand on the part of their mother, to hormonally crazed behaviour? I know of one young savant who already dispenses information, with a wink, to his friends as to what his mother likes to binge on before her period. Chocolate, what else? (Never mind, said a friend, when I told her about this kid, he'll make some woman very happy one day.)

Then there are the husbands whose datebooks are carefully marked with their wives' cycles (all the better, says the cynic in me, to plan that out-of-town trip). Many men do not want to know about PMS. Whenever those initials are said aloud, these men look pained or fearful or, if they are brave, bored.

Like many other recently recognized medical conditions, PMS may have been subjected to media overkill—it's everywhere! But the fact is, it *is* everywhere: the Canadian Medical Association says 90 per cent of women are affected by PMS at some time.

Maybe it seems more severe because we are living lives in which stress has been raised to Olympian levels. Some of us guzzle coffee to stay awake, and most of us put our own needs for rest and relaxation last. It is no wonder that with this kind of tension, our aging bodies get crankier. We need to acknowledge this—and not just in a greeting card that speaks more to male paranoia than it does to female discomfort.

On the other hand, one of the great delights of having more female comics around is that they are dealing with what was once unmentionable. On a recent Royal Canadian Air Farce show, comedienne Luba Goy, pretending to be a native-rights activist,

Susan Born-With-An-Attitude, is asked by a talk show host how she is today: "I am an oppressed minority, I'm a woman, and I'm retaining water. How do you think I am?" she snaps. Mini-pad humour is clearly big. But it is also a bit discomfiting: women who have fought hard for equality in private and public life have no desire to sabotage it all by insinuating that for a few days every month, the missile button needs to be locked away while Madam PM(s) gets over it. The truth is, in my years of covering politics, I've heard many more scary stories about off-the-wall male politicians (*and you know who you are*) pushing people over tables or melting down in the corridors of power than I have about women losing it because of their menstrual cycles.

What is really needed here is genuine understanding and good-humoured support on the part of men. And if they throw in a decent back massage they can avoid two or three days of relationship hell. But let's also keep those water-bloating jokes coming in. I laughed aloud not too long ago when I read of a female comic in a Toronto comedy club. During an aggressive rampage through the valley of the shadow of hormones, she was bothered by a male heckler. So she warned him: "I've got a cramp with your name on it." Perhaps male paranoia in this case is a good thing.

NOTES FROM THE MODERN NUCLEAR FAMILY LABORATORY

*A*re we a thoroughly modern family? A work in progress? A failed experiment? Some days we manage to be all three, as we limp along through the minefields of modern life. I read in the newspaper that in today's liberated family, the husband arranges for the baby-sitter as often as the wife does. Oops. Give my husband an F for failure to locate the family telephone book, let alone make the phone call. A television panel discussion informs me that the post-feminist man knows at all times whether there is enough milk in the refrigerator. Give him a C-. He knows when the fridge is empty, but he still forgets to bring home the milk.

On the other hand, he cleans up the kitchen better than I do, picks up clutter as much or more than I do, and spends a lot of his weekend doing things with the children, including highly evolved arts and crafts. (Mine are hands that have never touched papier-mâché paste, while his are hands that glory in mask-making or painting.)

And yet, if you called him up at work and asked him what the children's schedules were on that particular day, there would be a long pause. Whereas I know, down to the nanosecond, what they are doing and where they are supposed to be doing it. But I need to know what everyone is doing—it cuts down on the worry and inevitable guilt when I am away from the household or, more importantly, even when I am in it.

Linking guilt and working mothers is not only retro—it's wrong. All mothers, whether they have an outside job or not, feel guilty on one level or another; we are in the Olympics of guilt (I've never come in with less than a bronze). As a countermeasure, I try, once a day, to reassure at least one of my friends, as they do me, that she is a better mother than she thinks she is.

I know that to achieve a truly liberated household, women still have to cede more daily control and responsibility to their husbands, but in our home, that project is still in the early test-tube phase. (Give me a C-minus.) On a daily basis, with the intensity of an air-traffic controller, I oversee our household as well as do my outside work. Why me? My husband works longer hours than I do, but he is also less inclined to do some of the basic tasks. So, I manage all the doctor's appointments, and take most of the responsibility for arranging the children's social activities. Like many young children, they have social lives that are sadly over-orchestrated, for the simple reason that in our neighbourhood, we cannot allow them out to play freely, the way our mothers once opened the door, shooed us out and said, "Supper's at six. . . ."

As a consequence, what my mother notices as the main difference in my life today versus the life she led is the busyness of it all—children being picked up and delivered here and there with the precision of a space launch, professional work to be done, and on top of that, community obligations and a social life to be taken care of.

In some cases it is overwhelming, but it has its positive side: when I asked my mother recently what her motivations were for finally getting a job when my brother and I were ten and eleven, she said with a laugh, "To get out of the kitchen and keep my brain alive." My problem is how to get my mind out of overdrive.

What do our children observe about the roles my husband and I play at home? (Please God, don't let them remember us as Homer and Marge Simpson . . . .) When they look at their father, they see, at times, a man in a suit with a briefcase, but they also see a man who gardens and bakes a fabulous apple pie (for which, I might add, he gets a disproportionate amount of credit from older female relatives, wildly impressed with his dessert after I've put the rest of the meal together). As for me, I get a secret thrill each time my children are asked that ridiculous question, "What do you want to be when you grow up?" and they sometimes reply they want to be a writer like Mommy (when they don't want to be like their father or, much more to the point, "a rock star or a mountain climber").

When my daughter is trying to be grown up at the dinner table, she will turn to me, apropos of nothing, and say, "So, how's your work going?" and I think, she gets it, she will never have to be worried that I live through her, or be reminded that a human being needs both love *and* work to be happy. Now that's modern.

GUILT TRIP

*Y*ou would think the combined forces of liberalism and feminism over the past three decades would have deleted, or at least diluted, maternal guilt. Surprise surprise. The women I know who are mothers today carry around as much or more guilt than mothers in the past.

I hear it in their voices—those apologetic voices! A friend calling to invite my son to her son's eighth birthday party murmurs she's sorry she "didn't have enough time to do written invitations." She is an accomplished actor, a budding director, and a more than competent and loving mother to her two childen, one of whom is a regular visitor to our home and has shown no signs of deprivation on any front. He even has good table manners. Yet she sounds as if she thinks she should be charged with failing to provide the necessities of life. I tell her warmly to give herself a break, and then I wonder why it is so difficult for her (or any of us, for that matter) to do so. What is it that makes all of us feel, whether or not we work outside as well, that we just are not doing enough for our children?

The guilt of the working mother is easy to understand. After all, society did send us a message that it was all right to be a brain surgeon, but you better make bloody well sure your floors are clean and your kids are perfect, because if they're not, you will get the blame.

Out of this punitive environment, the superwoman myth was born. And those of us who were not pulling off the perfect dinner party *and* the challenging job *and* the happy and contented children lied about our lives—to society, to each other, and even to ourselves. But guess what? It didn't matter. Working mothers got blamed anyway for just about every disaster short of Chernobyl. In fact, some critics claim that working mothers have been responsible for a Chernobyl of the family—no less than the nuclear family meltdown. Feeling that you have single-handedly brought down society can actually add a little pizzazz to one's everyday life. However, there are a lot of us to feel guilty together: the majority of women with children at home now work in full- or part-time positions.

Consequently we have exposed the myth of the superwoman, and the acknowledged reality today is that most women's jobs are not about daytimers, briefcases, and board meetings; they are about meeting the mortgage payments or supporting two children on the salary of a secretary. It's about having to work—and doing the best you can.

Yet there is still more than enough guilt to go around, and no end of people who reinforce it—people who should know better. One of my friends who stays at home told me that a teacher, a few years ago, said approvingly to her, "You can tell the children whose mothers are at home—their clothes are ironed." Comments like this used to send a working mother into orbit—or more likely down into the basement at 11 PM to ferociously iron her daughter's sweatpants.

Children's birthdays, for obvious reasons, provide major opportunities for guilt. There are either tired, busy women buying store-bought cakes for their kids and feeling compelled to apologize even to the cashier at Loblaws, or conversely, tired busy women working feverishly until 1 AM to make the perfect theme cake. (And then there are the ones who serenely have it all under control at least a day before, which of course pops another guilt vein in the rest of us.) I swear, either I or someone I know will one day crack under the strain and, instead of writing Happy Birthday Mikey or whomever in bright icing, will defiantly write on her kid's cake: "*I am so a good mother!*"

Another great source of guilt-mongering, I am sorry to say, is our mothers. "I'm going away to do a course," says one friend, "and my mother makes me feel like Anna Karenina—oh God, you're leaving the family!"

I lucked out in this department. My mother has done more to bolster my sometimes shaky sense of being a good mother than anyone else. Once, when one of my children was exhibiting behaviour that I feared could lead, in adulthood, to a permanent place on the Ten Most Wanted list, I sobbed to her that maybe I should not have been working part-time all these years. "Don't be ridiculous," she said, "your children get lots of attention."

Friends of mine have pleaded with me to rent my mother out, or even to give them her phone number. But I sometimes wonder whether the reason she is so forgiving and supportive of me is precisely because she feels guilty about her own lapses in motherhood—guilt that from my grown-up vantage point is unnecessary, but that she is nonetheless honest enough to admit to. She makes me realize that it does not matter what era we are living in. Short of giving them one of our kidneys, we all feel we haven't done enough for our children. And even then, can't you just hear one mother saying, "I should have given him the *other* one."

TO HAVE AND HAVE NOT

I am with a friend in her sun-filled kitchen one Sunday afternoon. We are drinking tea and talking about our lives. She is baking a cake, and deftly carries on with the mixing and blending as the conversation veers from hopes and dreams to should-have-dones, along with the occasional pause for serious fashion advice.

There are many similarities between us—we are both writers, both domestic creatures. The purchase, of just the right flannel sheets, say, can give each of us a frisson of joy that is mystifying to those who don't worship at the shrine of comfort and warmth. The great difference between us is that I have children and she does not. In other words, she gets to lick the batter spoon herself.

Nothing so defines a woman in life as the decision to have children. Not marriage, not choice of career, not even sexual preference any more. But whether or not she is a mother, with all its joys, terrors, limitations, and intense preoccupations, can still set up the great divide, a divide that women who are friends, sisters, colleagues, bosses, and employees struggle every day to bridge.

I have cried with friends over their miscarriages and futile visits to fertility clinics. They have, at no small emotional cost, joyfully welcomed my own children into the world. I have respected those other friends who, after careful consideration, have decided not to have children. In return, they have not only empathized with my struggles as a mother, but have consistently dazzled my kids. (My children, with great savvy, always tell me my non-mother friends are "way more fun.") And I have understood when a few of them have just drifted, unable to make a decision one way or another, until finally, in their late forties, there is no more talk of fertility.

Yet despite this attempt at empathy, there are days when it feels as though we are living in separate countries.

In my country, phone conversations are often punctuated by desperate hissed asides such as "Do that again and there will be a *serious* consequence" and "Can you *not* let me have even a five-minute conversation with a friend?" while the caller from that other country waits in tactful or impatient (and believe me I can tell the difference) silence. In my country, "I had a bad day at school" takes precedence over "My career is going down the toilet," at least until bedtime. And in my country, Ritz Bits are sometimes considered an acceptable hors d'oeuvre.

When I think of that other country, I am occasionally guilty of big-time sins: let's start with envy—of those impulsive weekend getaways, of the luxury of being able to work without interruption. And then, paradoxically, there is pity: "Oh God, their lives must be so empty." And finally there is resentment: "She thinks *she* has stress? Try having a deadline *and* a child who is throwing up all night and then give me a call."

In return, my childless friends, single or in relationships, have revealed a few dark reactions to my life. That big *F* for Family sign glows bright on the relationship highway. It says check in here, and you need never worry again about what to do on the weekend, or even for the rest of your life. And so, I hear envy: "Oh, your house is so lively . . ." And paradoxically, there is pity: "I couldn't help noticing when I was over that all you did was jump up and down and fetch things for everyone." And finally, resentment: "What do you know about loneliness and wondering who will be with you in your old age?"

There is also the thorny issue of regret. I have never heard a woman say publicly, or even privately, that she regrets having children. My own imagination, for example, is quite capable of delivering the perfect child-free weekend. But I cannot imagine not having had my children. It would involve breathing differently. Or maybe not breathing at all.

On the other hand, most of the women I know who could not or did not have children have expressed a little or a lot of regret at not having had the experience of motherhood. Even this friend, in her sun-filled kitchen, wonders what if . . .

The next time we get together, we are in my kitchen, and she has just blown in to borrow a pair of earrings for a big night out with a new man. With great feeling, she tells me that she loves her life— its freedom and possibilities. Its sense of excitement.

I check my own emotional pulse and I realize all I feel is pleasure for her. And I think, we should somehow honour this moment, however brief: two women, not only secure in their biological destinies, but taking delight in each other's lives. That great divide has simply melted away.

THE REAL JUGGLING ACT

*T*hose of us who are married, with children, and still living with our original spouse (and mine is very original), may one day soon be a minority in the great tableau of North American living arrangements. Other families are fast choosing—or having thrust upon them—a variety of alternative living situations.

I think of this sometimes when I am full-tilt into my rant: "My husband's not home tonight, the dishwasher's *broken*, the kids are *off the wall, I'm tired . . .*"

What I think of most, is how do single parents do it? They have no back-up, no spousal shoulder to cry on (or to frostily ignore if the domestic tension level is high), no second pair of hands. Most of them are burdened with heightened financial worries and, at the very least, the usual complement of concerns about their kids.

Single mothers (and fathers, if they are the ones primarily on deck) have to summon the strength to work all day, come home at night to feed the kids, help them with their homework, put them to bed, then get their house in order, and then, if it's possible, retrieve what's left of the evening for themselves. By themselves.

They manage because they have to, but the cost to their emotional well-being is high. From what I've seen, their self-esteem suffers and anxiety levels soar when the media report that children from single-parent families are doing less well at school and in social situations than children who come from so-called "intact" families. There is a punitive air to these articles, as if to say, "You should have thought of this before you ended up single." As if many of them had not agonized over leaving abusive or intolerable situations. As if many of them had not been left in the lurch by partners who didn't care enough to stick around. As if many of them had not chosen what, for their children, would have to be a better way of life than what they had.

Some single mothers are lucky enough to have extended family support, others have good friends who fill the breach. Few are relatively affluent. And virtually all the women I know who came to be single mothers, whether by choice or by chance, admit they are engaged, every day, in a herculean struggle to stay on top of what life demands of them. But that doesn't necessarily lead to regret. In fact, says a friend, the one thing that perks her up if she suddenly feels overwhelmed is the realization, "*At least I'm not with him.*")

One woman, separated with two children, told me tartly that if she were filling out a job application, the first job experience she would put on her résumé to demonstrate her managerial skills would be "single parent of two." Would anybody in a position to hire her get it? A married father I know, whose wife went away for a week, also told me, after spending that week doing every single thing that needed to be done in their household, including nearly having a nervous breakdown dealing—or not dealing, as it turns out—with a plumbing emergency, that he thought "only single parents should be allowed to run the country."

My favourite single-mother story concerns a woman I met at a school banquet. I'd seen her around—she has children the same age as my own. Once I bumped into her at Loblaws, when she was slinging groceries into her cart and throwing out a few wisecracks about child-care difficulties. She's a medical professional, with no support—financial or emotional—from her ex-spouse. Each day, every day, those children are solely her responsibility.

I questioned her closely about how she put her life together. Her children had a part-time baby-sitter, she said, but she had scheduled her hours to pick them up after school. And what about mealtimes? I asked. Do you have the energy to prepare dinner and deal with two lively kids after running your own clinic every day?

"Well," she said, "I juggle." "Oh, we all juggle," I replied, a little disappointed she had used that overworked word. "No," she said, "you don't understand, I *juggle*." And then, she confessed she had taken a juggling course, and while her children ate promptly at six (when she herself wasn't quite ready to eat) she performed juggling tricks for them.

To me, it was a powerful image—this woman throwing pins up in the air while her children watched between mouthfuls of macaroni. After that, she said, she would have a glass of wine and a little dinner, and all three of them would feel refreshed.

I think of her often as the family-values debate continues unabated, and those reports about children of divorce get more and more punitive. I think of her, too, when I get poisonous letters, like the one from a married mother who wrote to tell me to shed no tears for single mothers, because, after all, they were simply "sluts who have partied too long." This woman who wrote was very angry, primarily because, as she saw it, her role, with a live-in but basically unsupportive spouse, was so much harder.

The irony is that this woman who so virulently condemns single mothers is close to that line herself. Minus her man—through death or divorce—she's there. And then it will be her turn to juggle.

DO LESBIANS HAVE MORE FUN?

I went out to dinner recently with a friend whom I hadn't seen for more than a decade. She is a gorgeous, lively woman who, when I first met her, had been living with a male colleague of mine. Since then, she has crossed the gender Rubicon, and has subsequently been involved in several long-running lesbian relationships. Over dinner, she told me this story:

She and her current female partner recently threw a party at which only one heterosexual couple showed up. My friend, in her role as hostess, approached the lone straight woman in the room and asked her if she was having a good time. The woman smiled and replied, "I've never seen so many happy women!"

I laughed when I heard this story, and I have been amused by the response I get when I tell it to different people. My gay women friends hoot with laughter that has a slight "nyah nyah nyah, see what you're missing" quality to it. My straight women friends laugh too, or groan and say wistfully, "Of course . . ." (which, roughly translated, means "Oh, to be free once and for all of those male/female struggles"). And my straight men friends greet it either with stony silence or a sarcastic "Thanks for sharing that."

All these responses make me wonder whether there is such a

thing as a sexual or relationship utopia. Whenever I get together with my close female friends, say on a weekend trip, or a long house visit, we always joke about how smoothly things run when there are two women around. We need a salad dressing for dinner and . . . it gets made in a twinkling! The kids get restless and . . . one woman or the other immediately senses the problem and sets them up with Junior Scrabble! There is always someone to talk to, someone who is actually listening! And, oh joy, the woman who is the hostess gets up in the morning to find that her friend has already emptied the dishwasher from the night before! This causes the woman whose dishwasher it is to feel grateful out of all proportion, and to muse wryly or even bitterly that when there are two women on the case, *things get done magically without having to ask anyone through gritted teeth to do them!*

"I should be married to you, we have so much fun," more than one female friend has joked to me, and we both know there is not a scintilla of sexual innuendo in the remark. It would just be . . . more relaxing. There'd be more laughs. We could trade clothes.

But after a little independent polling, I of course discover what most thoughtful people of all sexual persuasions know already. Same-sex relationships—be they between men or women—are as loaded with *Sturm und Drang* as straight relationships. And not only that, they are fraught with some of the same dreary issues: control and power, jealousy, fear of aging, of losing your looks.

I asked a gay woman I know whether it matters to be good-looking in her community, and she said yes, absolutely. It seems the moment eros enters the scene, the laws of the sexual jungle, however cruel and unfair, can apply, no matter what your sexual inclination. So older gay men are afraid of being left by their younger, more attractive partners, and hot-looking lesbians are in demand on Saturday nights.

And then there is domestic life. If you ask straight women about the ongoing struggles in their relationships, most would put sharing the household duties near the top of the list. Are gay women any different?

"I won't let her put the dishes in the dishwasher because she stacks so lousy," says one gay friend. "Still, the least she could do is take them out. But, I get up in the morning and no-o-o they're still in there. What I do then," she continues, "is try for an orderly discussion, but we are not above frozen silences and hurled accusations that I am carrying more of the domestic load than she is." (And they don't even have rigidly defined gender roles to blame this on.) On a more serious domestic note, another gay friend checks in with a story about the difficulty she has getting access to the child she and her former female partner raised together.

During that restaurant dinner with my friend, she announced she was deliriously happy with her new mate. But then she added that her last girlfriend had been kind of closed down emotionally. And the one before that had tried to burn down the house when the relationship ended.

Hmm. Love, passion, rejection. *Arson.* Child custody. Boredom, lack of communication, trying to work your way through conflicts. And a dishwasher that always and forever needs emptying. I believe it is called being human.

VIEW FROM THE DECK

*E*very marriage has its major conflicts—the ones that threaten to blow it out of the water. And then there are the minor ones—the ones that crop up year after year as insistent reminders that no matter how much you love each other, you really are very separate people with sometimes diverging interests. Into this second category in my marriage falls the problem I've come to call bungee jumping vs. reading the *New Yorker*.

Simply put, my husband is a more physically active person than I am, and he regards weekends and summer vacations as opportunities to be lively in a variety of appallingly hearty ways—hiking, swimming, cycling, and canoeing, to name a few. I, on the other hand, regard those same time periods as windows for heavy leisure—I'm talking reading good books or magazines, listening to music, schmoozing with my friends, drinking a lot of coffee and appreciating the great indoors or, on a sunny day at the cottage, the view from the deck.

My children have of course made a serious dent in my pursuit of inactivity—or the contemplative life, as I like to call it. Now, I willingly (well, almost) go for a moderate bicycle ride with them, or a walk in the forest, or a paddle-boat ride (I like those boats because they have a place for my coffee mug), just so long as I can get back afterward to lying around reading magazines or listening to great music.

However, I do have unlimited physical energy for a few choice activities—including helping my children clean their bedrooms, dancing to good rock and roll, or shopping. Some friends claim my best sport is whitewater window shopping, in which I portage tirelessly from one store to the next, stopping only for a cappuccino. It's called urban body work.

But I loathe and abhor two or three so-called "fun" activities layered together—if I had wanted to be so engaged I would have taken a cruise and reported for shuffleboard at 9 AM followed by the hula-hoop contest on the third deck at 10. I get hostile at the mere suggestion of a highly scheduled leisure activity plan.

When my husband plans a breathtaking array of activities— "Let's cycle the boardwalk, come back for lunch, and then go to that pool with the water slide . . ."—I start to hyperventilate, thinking to myself, if I say yes to the bicycle trip in the morning, can I miss the water slide in the afternoon and then get away with playing only a few innings of baseball after dinner? That will hold them off. . . . But it does require the kind of strategy that those who are involved in the Middle East peace talks would appreciate. If I'm not vigilant here, it will soon be bungee jumping, and I will die.

Having kids who are six and eight as opposed to toddlers has made it easier on me—my husband now has other avid company for these excursions. But the flip side of this is that I always feel a bit wistful as I watch them go off together, and a bit lonely until they return with tales of multi-pool lengths and hiking prowess. The tape that says a family should play together repeats in my head, and I want to be with them, preferably nicely turned out in Gap hiking shorts . . . until I suddenly imagine myself out of breath and feeling like strangling their father as he pushes us to go that extra mile. I have even stooped so low as to compare him, in a guttural snarl, to the Great Santini, the bullying father of the movie and book who forces his adolescent kid to shoot baskets until he is in tears. But in fact, he is merely a joyful outdoorsman, the world's tallest boy scout, and our children love it—love the activity, the challenge, the fun.

Sometimes, even I love it. Nothing can give you the glow that good exercise can, and paddling a canoe on a crystalline northern lake with your loved ones is one of the great spiritual adventures open to Canadians.

Besides, I truly don't want them to be like I was—afraid of athletic activity because I simply was not very good at it. While there is no evidence to suggest this fear robbed me of a place on the Olympic gymnastics team, overcoming it in my childhood might have lessened the inner conflict I feel when the rallying cry is "Let's take a hike!" as opposed to, say, "Let's read decorating magazines!"

On the other hand, whose vacation is this, anyway?

QUEEN OF THE ROAD

*W*hat were vacations like when I was single? Well, of course, they were filled with wild adventure and mad, impetuous behaviour. Why, I remember that time in Oaxaca, Mexico. . . . If I close my eyes, I can see myself as I once was, twenty-four and fearless, sitting in the *zocalo*, wearing a straw hat, writing in my journal, and . . . pretending to be Malcolm Lowry's good sister. (I just couldn't drink anything strong in the hot sun.) Okay, maybe that's not the best example of wild and impetuous. Then there was that road trip along the Riviera with a close friend—the one where we took so many suitcases we basically spent most of our holiday changing our outfits . . . hmm.

Surely there was a time of high adventure and low romance (or vice versa) in my travelling past. Wait, it's coming to me . . . I did do some intrepid exploring, but that was when I was a news reporter. It was only when I had the legitimacy of a notebook, or a terse directive from a take-no-prisoners editor, that I was able to live large on the road.

We're talking excitement! Once, I even chartered a small plane to fly into a town in the Northwest Territories to cover a labour dispute. I remember the pilot—Bob, or Bill, or was it Billy Bob—shaking his head and saying reluctantly, "It looks like a storm up there," and me, with a husky, commanding tone to my voice, replying, "Let's try it, Billy Bob. If it gets bad, we can always turn back."

Flash forward to one husband, two kids, and a couple of decades later as, on the road again, I worriedly look for turn-off signs on an American turnpike that will lead us to the cleanest possible gas station washroom—how about one with security guards and iron bars on the door? Why do I get the sinking feeling that motherhood has rendered me even more timid about travelling than I was before?

Later, after spending the night at a Marriott Hotel ("children under six eat free!"), my husband looks dejected as we are repacking the car. "What's your problem?" I ask.

"It's like travelling with a seventy-year-old," he moans. "You don't want to take any chances."

I'm hurt. "Just because I wouldn't let you order fresh orange juice," I whine. "Well, it didn't *come* with the mini-breakfast buffet."

He says it isn't just that, more a general feeling of my being buttoned-down, like my insistence, the night before, on staying cloistered inside our hotel rather than taking two tired kids out to explore beautiful downtown Pittsburgh. Never mind that I can calibrate, to the exact second, when my children are about to have nervous breakdowns in tandem.

Still, despite my superior knowledge of the disasters that can happen to a family on the road vs. my husband's touching desire to have an adventure or two, I had to admit I had become . . . what's the opposite of death-defying . . . life-defying?

Moreover, I know that I cannot entirely blame nine years of motherhood for my timorousness. Having young kids has simply finished the job by injecting me with that most human of all obsessions: I desperately want them to be safe, so I batten down my own hatches. Of course, every parent can also spot the paradox here: I also take for granted that, despite being a travel wimp, I could, if called upon to defend my children from physical harm, rip someone's arm off at a moment's notice.

We are contemplating another road trip. I can see it all unfolding—suitcases crammed to the max, back seat of the car looking like a travelling art studio cum grocery store, with crayons (and crackers), markers (and munchies), paper (and no, Emily, you cannot take your entire stuffed animal collection, there just isn't room).

Up front, we adults will have our trusty maps, our coffee, and some really good tapes. (One of the great watershed moments of parenthood is the day you realize you need never listen to Sharon, Lois and Bram in the car again.)

This time, I am determined that things will be different. All I have to do is . . . relax, and practise saying "What a fabulous idea!" to my husband's life-threatening suggestions. Should we stop and look at that huge snapping turtle in the middle of the road? *What a fabulous idea!* Pull over to clamber up that mountainside? *What a fabulous idea!* Take a detour to try that waterpark with the slide that looks as though it could put the entire family in traction? *What a fabulous idea!*

I am going to celebrate the joys of the open road! Embrace the possibility of real, true adventure. Let my inhibitions blow in the breeze. Besides, as I said to Billy Bob that time in the far north, if it gets bad, we can always turn back.

LIFE'S A BEACH BOOK—AND THEN YOU DIET

*W*hat is summer about if not the serious pursuit of pleasure reading? Imagine relaxing on a screened-in porch on a sultry afternoon, or lounging down at the beach, with a delicious sense of anticipation as you finally crack the cover of that best-seller you've been hungering after. But suddenly you're suffering from a case of literary ennui. Are you exhausted by all those tracts about gender warfare? Cranky from the dozens of smug self-help books? Tired of wearing surgical gloves to turn the pages of the latest celebrity tell-all?

Me too. So, I've packed my own little beachbag of books for you, books that dazzle, surprise, inform, or delight, but never ever leave you with the feeling that civilization as we know it is over. Books that tell it like it should be.

GENDER BENDERS

Backsplash——The ultimate feminist tour de force: how North American women are the victims of a male conspiracy designed to keep women decorating their homes, exhausting them with day-long searches for the perfect Italian tile, when they could be finding the cure for cancer. You'll never go shopping again. (But just in case you do, the index lists great tile outlets.)

Ironing John——Sensitive and smart advice by a male therapist and closet organizer, primarily targeted toward heterosexual men who are slobs; shows them step by step how they can keep their closets in order, whatever or whoever is in them.

Men Are from Mark's (Work Wearhouse); Women Are from Eaton's——An astute analysis of the difference between Canadian men and women by tracking their shopping habits, eh.

SPIRITUALITY

Crossing the Threshold of Hype——Pope John Paul real and up-close about his life in the Vatican; admits he has never been allowed to order in pizza, and also confesses he made a mistake about this women in the church business, and really hopes the next Pope is a woman, possibly Madonna.

Braced by the Light——One mother shares her compelling account of a not-so-rare "near-life" experience in which, bathed in sweat after working all day, throwing dinner on the table, and driving two kids to soccer practice, she is jolted awake in her parked car in the community centre parking lot by a strange light, while the words "You call this a life?" spring spontaneously to her lips.

POLITICAL PURSUITS

On The Take-Out——Intrepid investigative journalist Stevie Cameron goes south, and produces a waistline-popping exposé of Bill Clinton's junk food habits; a real whopper, dripping with facts.

Neo-Connivers!——A reassuring field guide for those alarmed by the newest generation of conservative thinkers. These little crit-ters, raised and cosseted in various elitist nests, are now claiming entitlement to all the best society has to offer, while promoting capital punishment for just about everyone else. Turns out, apart from their distinctive warble ("Mine! mine!"), they're pretty harmless, and tend to wear themselves out if allowed to roam free through the media.

CRIME/ETIQUETTE

Raging Houseguest——Brian "Kato" Kaelin offers a spirited but practical collection of do's and don'ts for houseguests caught in tricky situations. The key, he says, is to be genuinely helpful—remember to turn off the jacuzzi, keep your statements to the homicide police simple and consistent, and get yourself a decent agent.

SELF-HELP

So Far Down the Road Less-Travelled That I Can't Remember Why the Caged Bird Sings——A female therapist/poet/travel agent suggests that running away is still the only tried and true method of dealing with life's problems; includes twenty-five fabulous weekend getaways.

FOR KIDS

Where's Forrest?——Forrest Gump replaces Waldo as the politically correct image to locate in various exotic locales.

HORROR

Splasher: Anne Rice creates an evil toddler vampire who wreaks havoc at the local wading pool. Gruesome fun for all ages.

POETRY

Morning, Afternoon, and Evening in the Heavily Mortgaged House——Margaret Atwood lyrically connects with *all* Canadians in this new, humane collection of poetry.

COOKBOOKS

The No-Food Cookbook——It's the only way left to ensure that nothing fat-inducing, artery-clogging, or heart-stopping passes your lips. Filled with interesting three-dimensional cardboard designs you can cut out and press to your lips. Scent strips included (the tuna casserole scent strip might be a bit much in the hot sun), plus a coupon for Loblaws' latest President's Choice Sauce, "Memories of Cooking."

And finally,

DIETING (Did you really think I'd let you go to the beach without at least one book about body image?)

Stop the Inanity!——One woman who doesn't have short, spiked, white-blond hair tells how she consumed twice her body weight in nachos over the past year, and was still able to fit into her size 10 (okay 12) Land's End striped bathing suit (readers can send away for photographic proof if desired).

Now that's what I call feel-good reading.

A SEPTEMBER SERENITY
PRAYER

*S*chool looms. The summer ends, and any glow of well-being will soon be replaced by an almost brutal sense of running as fast as we can. New jeans and haircuts, sign-ups for extracurricular activities, school shoes, classroom blues, binder hues, school schedules, work schedules, and all those infernal lessons—piano and life.

I take a deep breath, and urge myself and others on, but I wish there was something like the serenity prayer to gear me up for the struggle. You know, the one that goes: "God, grant me the serenity to accept the things I cannot change, the courage to change the things I can, and the wisdom to know the difference."

My first problem is, I can't quite think of a household deity higher than myself to pray to, but I'll give it a shot:

Oh Great Goddess of Life, Love, Learning, and Laundry, help me to be a better mother this school year. Help me to, as my husband never tires of urging me, "lighten up," to go with the flow (to which my most belovedly acerbic friend replied to *her* husband, "You don't understand, I *am* the flow!").

Anyway, Great Goddess, help me, in my daily delirium, to understand that we have slain the superwoman dragon—she is dead

dead dead—and we do not have to be perfect as we stagger through our action-packed lives.

Enable me first of all, Goddess, to understand that having healthy food in the fridge at all times is a wonderful thing to strive for, but that some nights, children can learn a great deal about how lucky they are from eating Cheez Whiz on toast.

Help me, too, to have enough teenage baby-sitters on hand to actually have a life, and help me to not immediately freak out the next time I ask my daughter how the new boy baby-sitter was, and she replies, "Not good. He tied me to the bed when I wouldn't go to sleep." Maybe all he needed was a little talk about boundaries.

Goddess, in matters of health and hygiene, let me be so well-organized that I already have a bottle of Nix creme rinse on hand for those moments when my children say, "Mom, my head feels awfully itchy."

As for school responsibilities, Goddess, help me not to hyper-ventilate when one of my kids announces, at 7 PM that he has a project due the next day, in French, on the history of llamas. Enable me to understand that other parents, too, sigh long and hard about homework, and that it is normal not to want to list the ten provinces and their capitals after a hard day at the office.

Goddess, reassure me that I am not a bad person just because I duck into the school washroom when I see the chair of the PTA coming toward me with the volunteer list in her hand. Let me also not feel I am a threat to civilized society because the words "bench-marks" and "whole language" make me want to throw spitballs at the teachers. And grant me a sense of compassion, Great Goddess, when the first school newsletter comes home with three spelling errors in it.

In schoolyard matters, Goddess, let me not overreact when one of my daughter's friends calls her a "rotten hunk of baloney"; and help me, please, to see the educational value of the joke my ten-year-old son brings home: "What did the dick say to the condom?" "Cover me—I'm going in!"

Goddess, I know I am asking a lot here, but grant me the sheer physical stamina it takes to go back-to-school clothes shopping with my daughter, and let me not shriek, "It doesn't even fit you properly!" when she tries on an oversize and hideously expensive jacket and says, "Mom I love it!" Let me not sob when my son says in an elegiac tone, "Mom you know that new Nike sweatshirt you just bought me, the one you paid $40 for?"

Goddess, give me a sense of proportion, too, about extracurricular activities, and please let me not feel hopelessly inadequate when another mother triumphantly tells me she managed to get her Tyler signed up for madrigal singing, karate, and calligraphy—and that's just Saturday morning.

And oh Goddess, let me be patient when my husband asks me, only half kidding, what grades the children are in this year (what's a little detail, for a big-picture man?). Let me then be humble, when I, too, have trouble with that. (It can't be Grade 5, *can* it?)

And finally, Goddess, let me remember each and every day what it was like to be a kid going back to school.

Nasty.

THAT'S ENTERTAINMENT

*O*ne minute, we think it is a wonderful idea. We picture ourselves so pathologically organized that Martha Stewart will
be begging for tips, spiffily dressed, and applying the finishing
touches to a living room warmed by the glow of the fire, ready to
welcome seventy guests. Our dining-room table is heaped with
food—potato latkes and smoked turkey—the menorahs are ready to
be lit by eager childish hands, the children drift by, polished and
buffed. Aah. The holiday party.

The next minute, the vision changes to something resembling a
suicide pact, with condiments: two frantic people clawing in the
cupboard for more green garbage bags as platters empty at an alarm-
ing pace, slabs of smoked turkey lie greasily on the couch, and all of
the interesting conversation is just out of earshot. Somewhere in
the house, a child is throwing up.

The urge to give a holiday party is profound. The commitment
to carrying through, though, requires nerves of steel. We began giving a large Chanukah party years ago, and it became an instant tradition, with people asking pointedly in early fall whether we had
picked a date for it yet.

But the last one we gave reached a critical mass that unnerved
me. At the height of it, I stood in my crowded kitchen, surveying

the chaos, watching my husband scrape plates in a frenzy as people in nice clothes milled about, and I thought, "I've lost the thread here." (There is probably a medical term for this kind of party-induced vagueness.) And although many of the guests later insisted they'd had a good time, I ended up with a serious case of post-party letdown. I lay on the couch waiting for the dish-rental people to come pick up the lipstick-smeared wine glasses, morosely pondering the meaning of lifestyle.

So we put the party on hold. The recession was a good (and legitimate) excuse to cut back, while we examined the problems of having a wonderful but very large extended family that leaves little room for our friends. My sister-in-law, who hates large parties, suggested only half-humorously that we stagger the guest list—people could come on a three-year rotating basis—and she was willing to wait a few years. But try explaining that to your mother.

Another friend hinted that the party perhaps did not mean as much to my non-Jewish friends. *Au contraire*, it is my non-Jewish friends who really like to see those menorahs lit, and besides, that would mean disinviting half of our family. Try explaining *that* to your mother.

During these last two party-free years, my husband and I have congratulated each other: "Thank God we're not giving the party with this (laryngitis) (deadline) (bad mood) we've got."

But secretly I missed it—the pre-party planning and work, the excitement, the curtains-up moment when the first guest arrives, and of course the feeling of indescribable happiness that comes over you when your home is filled with people you love, all of whom seem to be having the time of their lives.

I even missed the dangerous elements—that panic just before the doorbell rings that people were actually going to *starve* in our house, never mind that I almost got a hernia lugging the food to the table. The fear that the multi-menorah lighting might get out of hand and resemble the California brush fires. And then there is another unpredictable force of nature, my father-in-law, who spent one party standing in the corner counting the number of latkes consumed by each person. One hapless accountant ate over a dozen of the crispy little potato pancakes that are traditional fare at Chanukah. ("Oh boy, he was having himself a picnic," muttered my father-in-law darkly.) For his own personal safety, the gobbler was not invited back.

I even missed our pre-party fight. What? There is a couple out there who don't snap at each other before they are about to feed seventy people? I do not wish to hear about it.

It used to seem that every child at the party (and there were about twenty-five of them) was under the age of five. This year, though, my children and all the children we know are older. Instead of hiring baby-sitters to control them, a couple of cool videos would do the trick. And with the money saved on sitters, voilà!—we could hire professional kitchen help, people you pay to stand around the kitchen looking vague on your behalf.

I think of the people I can count on—my mother, who remembers not only all my friends' names, but the projects to which their egos are so tremulously tied; and my mother-in-law, who in her spare time (if she had any) could give guest lectures at any of the world's best hospitality schools.

So it all seems doable again. All we have to do is make that commitment. Call those party-rental people for the dishes. Order that turkey. Count the wine glasses.

And maybe look in the Yellow Pages, under Nerves of Steel.

LONG DAY'S JOURNEY INTO KITCHEN CLEAN-UP

*O*ne of the best family dinners I ever experienced was the time the adults in my husband's family catered an intimate sixtieth birthday dinner for my mother-in-law. We wore black tie, we hired a pianist to play Gershwin, and we were all on our best behaviour. But what pushed the dinner into genius was that my mother-in-law knew instinctively that her role was not to be the passive centre of attention (passivity, in her case, being a gene that was apparently bred out at least a generation before). Instead, at the candlelit table, she movingly spoke of each of us, and what we meant to her. The glow lasted a long time.

One of the worst dinners, I'm sorry to say, was approximately the same set of characters, plus children, some of them annoyingly peevish, a hot night, the wrong topic for discussion (I can't remember if it was pay equity or affirmative action, but it certainly confirmed Gloria Steinem's tart theory that women grow more radical with age while men become more conservative). One man lost his temper, and at least one woman I know was hormonally challenged. Kids fidgeted, nobody seemed remotely interested in anything anyone else had to say, and all the strawberry shortcake in the world could not make it right. "Well, that was a disaster," said my husband amiably later.

It is certainly not news to anyone as we head into the entertaining season that the family get-together—with its potential for conflict and chaos, and enough neurotic undercurrents to bring you to your knees, is a challenge that some people look forward to almost as much as gum surgery.

We can rehash Tolstoy's brilliant axiom that all happy families are alike, and each unhappy family is unhappy in its own way, or we can cut straight to the chase—recalling the time Uncle Henry grabbed his brother around the neck, got him in a stranglehold, and yelled, "You are too a greedy bastard" while the cranberry sauce toppled off the table, or the time cousin Louise announced she was pregnant—by her brother-in-law—or merely, because not all of us are so obviously dysfunctional, the time your dweeby sister actually thought a can of toasted almonds was an adequate contribution to a dinner you had sweated over for two weeks.

I am a sucker for family gatherings. I get too excited about them, I work too hard at them, and then I sit there, either appalled or in heaven as they progress to their inevitable end. Some of these get-togethers last an entire weekend (if this is Saturday, it must be Aunt Sheila's) and not only involve far too many wardrobe changes, but can build to a major migraine, a profound insight into the family you belong to, or have married into, or a trial separation (you don't honestly think you're sleeping with me tonight after *that*?).

As I grow older, even setting the table for a family dinner takes on a certain poignancy. The extended family groans, shifts, and changes, through divorce, death, birth, and even—wonderfully—adoption, in ways we had never imagined. On my husband's side, Nanny's chair is empty, and in many families I know, relatives who once commanded the room with the sheer force of their personalities have been physically shattered in ways that make it hard to look at them and hard to look away.

Time plays amusing tricks as well: we who used to be the subversive element—snickering as the adults downed their furtive second (or fifth) drinks, or made yet another inane comment—have become the snickerees, while our children, edging into adolescence, practise their lip-curls and murmur "Oh, please" in our direction.

Through it all, my favourite family characters faithfully play their roles: there is my brother, who is so engagingly offensive that he can unite an entire dinner table against him, a certain brother-in-law who defuses many a family time bomb with a silly joke, a sister-in-law who generously keeps an eye out when I am the hostess, knowing I have a tendency to fade in the third act. (Dessert? What dessert?) There is of course my husband, who has been known to leap up from the table after being so silent he seemed in need of life support, and rush to play the piano. (Maybe that is his life support.)

I used to rail at the confusion of these dinners, long for something more sophisticated or laid back. But recently, I realized I was fooling myself and that it is the very noise! music! intrigue! pronouncements! announcements! cranky opinions! that engage me, along with the crapshoot itself. What will it be, triumph or disaster?

There is a wonderful passage in American author Anne Tyler's novel *Ladder of Years* in which an older man looks at a photograph of a table set for a family holiday celebration—"chair after chair after chair, silverware laid just so, even a baby's high-chair, all in readiness." The man, deep in his own family turmoil, contemplates this exquisite table, all ready and waiting for the family members to arrive and claim their places, and says, "I bet that's as good as it got, that day. From here on out, it was all downhill, I bet."

Maybe. But then again, maybe not. So, bring on Uncle Henry (there's one in every family). And, short of a fatal stabbing, give me anything at a family get-together, but don't give me indifference. In a pinch, I'll even take toasted almonds.

SELECTED STATES OF
MODERN LIVING

PURÉED

My sister-in-law and niece are driving in the car, and they become increasingly irritated by the erratic driving of the guy in front of them. He slows down, he speeds up, he seems to be half turned in his seat, his arm keeps coming up, what the hell is he doing? They pull alongside of him, and burst out laughing: he is driving with one hand, and in the other is a jar of baby food; he is actually feeding his infant child, strapped into a car seat in the back. Call it puréed rush hour.

CORDLESS

For me, the single most important invention of the last decade or so has been not the car phone but the cordless phone. Setting aside the time I came very close to accidentally throwing it into the washing machine along with the whites, it has given me freedom to make calls while doing several other things at once. I believe the dreary sociological term for this is multi-tasking (this is news for women?) but it really means my daily phone call to my mother usually takes place while I'm cleaning the kitchen. My mother, however delighted she is with my call, is nevertheless always a bit taken aback when she hears the sounds of those dishes being slammed

into the cupboards. Where she came from—in time and space—
one gave one's caller the courtesy of one's full attention. I keep
intending to try it some time. In the meantime, she continues to
ask pointedly, "What's that noise?" and I continue to answer defen-
sively, "Mom, I'm just emptying the dishwasher. I *have* to."

STRANDED

A friend called long-distance with the ultimate horror story—a
woman she knows with a high-powered job, a six-month-old baby,
and a four-year-old, finally arranges a four-day getaway in New York
with her husband. They have never left the children before. They
leave the nanny with the children and off they go on a Friday afternoon. On Saturday morning, the nanny, a 42-year-old woman, dies of
a heart attack while sitting in a chair. The baby is still in the crib. The
four-year-old didn't comprehend the nanny's anguished request to call
911. But a friend of the couple happens to drop in unexpectedly on
Saturday, finds the nanny dead, and the kids confused but unharmed.
There are two morals to the story, says my friend. Number one: if you
go away, always get someone to check on your kids, even when a baby-
sitter is looking after them. And number two: as soon as they can comprehend it, teach your children how and *why* to call 911. But if you
happen to be a pushover for maternal guilt and anxiety, there is also a
third: don't ever, ever leave home—it isn't worth it.

BUSY

My daughter springs the news on us, at the last minute, that she has
a cross-country running meet that day, and could we come. I
wince—my workload is ridiculously heavy, Martin has a morning of
appointments. He begins to furiously paw his briefcase. (I think we
get the point, Martin.) But there she is, looking down at her bowl,
saying, "I really want someone to be there for me." My heart melts.
Five years from now, who will care if my article was in on time? But
a little girl might remember a parent waving madly at the finish
line. Just as the music from *Chariots of Fire* begins to swell in my

head, my daughter adds, in a hey-that's-totally-cool kind of voice: "Tracy's parents can't go, of course. They're both lawyers." So what are we, chopped liver?

STRETCHED
Many educators and daycare workers are troubled about (and feel, viscerally) the level of stress in kids' lives today. Both of our children go, after school, to an in-school daycare that provides them with snacks, activities, and a remarkable level of warmth and support (and joy) from the staff. But I sometimes see, in the faces of Anne, the director, and Mary, the senior staff person in the centre, all the absorbed stress of the day. If it isn't coming from the kids, it's certainly coming from the parents as they arrive, many of them exhausted and brittle, to pick up their kids and to unload, as they sometimes do, their anxieties about their children or their life. Often, I wonder whether Anne and Mary just go home at night and sob. I know they felt like sobbing in the face of proposed government cutbacks: a full thirty per cent of their children are on subsidies and they don't know what will happen to these children after school if the money isn't there. At school end, every year, limp with gratitude (whatever we pay them, it isn't enough), we hand them modest gift certificates, or flowers, or aromatherapy bubble bath, and pray they will return in the fall.

Our school principal, new at the job and filled with energy and fresh ideas, told me that he sits at his desk and watches, from his window, the tired, tense faces of the parents picking up their kids at school. The faces do light up when they see their children—but the voices reveal the stress: "Hurry. We're late. Come on now, Mommy's tired. We're going home and [teeth gritted] that's a good thing."

OVERPROGRAMMED
The principal also sees some kids still at school between 6:30 and 7:00 at night—they've done an after-four class and now they're doing piano. They look exhausted. One day in the school yard, he

saw a little girl just lying down in the grass looking at a bug, and he thought, cloud study, every kid should do this. But every kid can't, and ironically, even their cloud study is overscheduled—one of my closest friends piled her kids into the car on a Saturday morning to go on a "fun" excursion to see a historical monument, and from the back seat, her youngest pleaded, "Mom, when do we get a day off?"

For many kids, the overprogrammed life changes when they slip into adolescence—otherwise known as perfecting the state of absolute passivity (especially if you're a boy). There should be a study that tells us whether kids who have had the daylights programmed out of them in their younger years are more active as teens—or the reverse. I talked to one teenage girl who, on a Sunday, had one activity after another—hockey followed by community league basketball followed by piano. I said, "When do you just have a good time?" And she replied, "You don't understand. The good time is whatever I'm doing."

UNDERNOURISHED

Food and modern life. It's a complicated relationship: going through the health food store, I pick up a loaf of white country bread because I don't have the time to sort through the various flax/seed/wheatgerm options and also, it seems as though it is the freshest. When I bring it home, the kids are so happy you would think I had put sugared donuts on the table. "Look!" yells my son excitedly, "it's white bread! Mom, thanks!" My daughter is equally delighted. "You're the greatest, Mom." So much for a decade of whole wheat.

There is a breakfast program operating at our school, and I have occasionally, along with the kids, gone in to staff the toaster. We turn out traysful of peanut butter and toast and it all gets eaten, some of it by children, including mine, who have clearly been fed once already at home. But there are children who come back for seconds and thirds, children who are truly hungry, and it is these children, without isolating them, we want to catch. Here we are, in the nineties, in a neighbourhood in which some kids set off for school from renovated houses and others from subsidized housing, and both sets of kids empty those trays.

Cruising down Bayview Avenue at 7 PM on a fall evening, it's dark with a hint of cold in it and we're coming from Hebrew lessons, when suddenly it occurs to me that I have no intention of cooking dinner. We can go to a real restaurant, and spend money on food the kids won't eat—or we can go to McDonald's. I don't even have to ask the kids what they would prefer. This McDonald's, in a fairly affluent neighbourhood, is bustling. Here comes a middle-aged gentleman in what can only be described as sage green lifestyle roughwear, and he looks tremendous. Over there, in the corner, sits another middle-aged couple—he's reading the paper and she's doing the crossword puzzle. "What's a four-letter word for legal document?" she asks him. I'm surprised by the number of childless customers. It would never occur to me to come here without children. A little girl in a dark green private-school uniform is scarfing a pizza while her father yacks on a cellular phone. A pretty young mother in blue jeans and denim top tries to get her little guy to stop fidgeting so she can feed him. A yuppie suit stares blankly across the room as he inhales his combo meal. And then of course there's us—tired, not saying much, we dip our chips into the paper cups of ketchup, and I am once again shocked at the tastelessness of the food. I also feel a mild flicker of fury at the wasted paper—a shiny, patterned paper box for the so-called "happy meal."

I remember, almost twenty years ago, when I was just out of university, a guy I knew who fancied himself to be a real trend-spotter said to me, "I'm gonna show you something that will blow your mind." He took me to the very first McDonald's in the area, and announced, "This is the future." Well, here I am, in a place that is too brightly lit, has no neighbourhood feel to it, no sense of time and place. But the slice of life is authentic, if not the slice of pizza. It does, in a way, define us all, hurtling toward the millennium on a cold autumn night.

D-I-V-O-R-C-E-D

Dropping the kids off at the first day of day camp last summer, I wait while my daughter boards the camp bus. "Are you going to be picking her up tonight?" the counsellor asks me. When I reply that I am, she says apologetically, "You'll need photo I.D." I look surprised, and she adds, "We just had too many problems with custody battles last year." Walking away on a bright, sunny morning, I feel sad for the kids who have to wait with a knot in their stomachs, wondering which parent is going to scoop them first, and then wondering if the other parent is going to be mad at them. Coming back at 4 PM though, I am appalled at the traffic jam created on the street as the bus idles and each and every parent's I.D. is checked. The effect of divorce on urban traffic flow.

Kids' social lives today resemble quiz shows—now let me see is Dana with her mother or father this weekend? If she's with her father, doesn't that mean she can't go cycling 'cause her bike is at her mother's? And her mother has currently gone back to court about her father, so should we just forget about calling her at her dad's? No, let's call her at her dad's . . . her dad's girlfriend is that neat lady who does balloon art . . .

I have a witty if somewhat cynical friend who likes to say that no self-respecting kid today has two natural parents living under the same roof. Her marriage is still intact, which is why, I guess, she's able to make such jokes . For the friends I know who struggle with joint custody arrangements, however cordial, the longing to be with their children never goes away and is always at odds with the reality—on the weekend you've got them, you're sick or you have a work deadline or there is nothing to do; on the weekend you don't have them, you sit alone miserable, wishing there were someone to make pizza for. It's that longing that gets in the way of life.

I once asked two pre-teen girls who were members of a softball team to tell me about themselves, and the first bit of information both of them volunteered was that their parents were divorced. More than one-third of Canadian marriages end in divorce, so it shouldn't be surprising that kids see it as relevant information. What gives one pause, though, is that they see it as absolutely defining information. "I don't see my dad all that much," one of them added. Divorce, for many kids, means entire relationships that once meant so much to them simply disappear. Picking up the kids at their daycare one night just before the Christmas holidays, we got talking in a group, about grandparents. Several kids were going off on vacations with, or to see, their grandparents. Except one little girl who announced, "My grandma lives in Saskatchewan, but I don't see her any more." End of story.

DISTURBED

I meet a music therapist at a party who works with disturbed or unhappy children, trying to give them, through music and rhythm, an outlet for their frustrations. "So many kids are unhappy today," she says flatly. Mainly she sees kids whose basic emotional needs are neglected: their parents—from all social strata—are too busy, too tired, or too stressed to meet them. These kids don't feel they are at the centre of anyone's existence. They don't feel they matter enough. It is ironic, the music therapist and I agree, that despite the emphasis and constant blah blah blah about self-esteem—in our society and in the schools—it is in such short supply among kids today.

REDEEMED

Lesley Krueger, the education columnist of *The Globe and Mail*, writes a thoughtful column one day about a book called *The Optimistic Child* by Martin Seligman (published by Houghton

Mifflin). Seligman castigates the self-esteem movement while offering advice that is so simple you wonder why it hasn't quite occurred to you—in order to build real self-esteem, you give your children opportunities to succeed, not chances to fail, and you don't praise them falsely. (Kids are smart enough to know when you're lying.) One of Seligman's key points is that self-esteem is not the forerunner to achievement, it is the result of it. I wonder, briefly, how that squares with our experience at the children's piano recital last spring. Their teacher, Chris, is extraordinary, and the program for the recital tells why: beside many of his students' names, there is a symbol indicating they have won scholarships, money, prizes, or ribbons. Most of the award-winners are Asian. I watch while their parents sit serenely, with dignified half-smiles on their faces, while their children rip through a complicated scherzo, and I wonder if it is a result of cultural difference that, when our two get up and, apart from competently performing their own pieces, charmingly play a simple duet—"Red River Valley"—Martin and I are obviously ecstatic, clapping vigorously, *yes! all right!* smiling and, okay, even waving. Are our standards lower? Or are we just more expressive?

What I find most touching, though, is that our children don't view it at all as a competition, they seem so rooted in their own performances, and so happy to have played well. Emily, who has had her hair braided with an intriguing crown intertwined with black ribbon, has a stately poise perched over the piano, and Jonathan seems full of confidence and good humour, even though he said later he was shaking. I felt so much love for them, pride in them, and joy coming from them. Later, we all—my mother, Martin, the kids, and I—celebrated at a pizzeria. Was it real self-esteem that was in abundant supply that night? I hope so.

On a Friday afternoon, I take my son to the Royal Conservatory of Music to try his Grade 3 piano exam. The waiting room is filled with nervous children and their anxious parents. Kids study their music books with stricken looks on their faces, as if to say *scales?*

why didn't I practise those scales more?, and their parents alternate between reassurance and their own looks of barely suppressed hysteria. Jonathan goes off when his name is called, turns back once, and gives me a wan wave. Waiting, I suck on candies, and think I can just hear the strains of what he is playing, and it sounds all right to me; but then I see a father, brow furrowed, ear cocked, and it's clear he thinks he hears his own child playing. His daughter, almost twelve, emerges first and announces flatly to him: "I blew the first piece." "And the sonata?" her father asks worriedly. The people in this room are of all skin colours and ethnic origins. They have only one thing in common—they are offering their children that chance to achieve. What is most poignant is that, because of the inadequacy of the public school system—and the vagueness of marking and therefore clearly recognizing real achievement—this is one of the few times our child has ever been clearly graded on anything. He comes out, like most every other kid, shaking his head and saying, "I blew it." But, after a milkshake and a half-hour's distance from his ordeal, he is all smiles. It's over. "Mom, when the envelope comes from the Conservatory," he tells me, "don't open it. I want to get the news first."

CONFUSED

I hear the sounds of a television program that seems a little too grown-up for the kids—when I come upstairs, they are both lying on the couch staring at the screen intently. I see a woman dressed in a white coat, and another woman lying on a hospital bed, who suddenly gets up and runs out of the room. "What gives?" I ask. "She was considering a breast reduction," says my nine-year-old son matter-of-factly without taking his eyes off the screen. Meanwhile, the woman in the white coat—the doctor I presume—is yelling after her, "If you don't do this, you'll have back pain for the rest of your life!" I leave, wondering how my children process such absurd information. What do they file it under? Breasts? Doctors? White coats? Back pain?

RESIGNED

A quote from a nine-year-old boy, at the dawn of his age of cynicism: "Mom, all Barney talks about is loving, caring, and sharing—when's he gonna get realistic?"

INFERIOR DECORATING

Now that my biological clock has stopped ticking (two school-age children with astoundingly definite personalities have taken care of that noise), and now that I've at least begun to face the possibility that I'm not going to win the Nobel Prize for literature, I've entered a new zone of longing, a new land of ambition and dreams. We're talking very nice Italian fabric. We're talking accent cushions. We're talking redecorating the house.

Last year, it was time. Actually, it was past time—the couches in our living room were ones I had bought when I was single. I had dated on those couches! In other words, they were very, very old. And our walls, well, they were all off-white with smudges and stains—eight years of vigorous childhood glaring at us no matter how low we kept the lights. And so I embarked on a serious journey, one that resulted in huge mood swings and great outlays of cash. And like Martin Luther King, I had a dream, only mine involved textured walls in the master bedroom.

There was just one problem. I didn't know where to start; I didn't know how to make a decision. I know women who have decorated entire houses in the time it takes me to select a plastic napkin holder for the kitchen table. I practically had to go on the couch to buy a couch. I brought home bagfuls of samples to show my husband

and children, I bribed friends to accompany me to fabric and furniture stores, I read decorator magazines religiously, somehow hoping it would all come together, and that I would turn into the kind of person who chooses brilliant couches (I did) and then triumphantly masters window treatments (I didn't).

Of course, I blame my mother. She taught me many useful things, but never once did she sit me down and tell me when roman shades were appropriate. And we have the bare windows to prove it.

Our walls fared better. For the painting, a close friend recommended Albert, with only one proviso: "He does a fabulous job but he likes to take his time." Albert, a pleasant-looking man in his fifties, came over, and I heard the angels singing. Here was no brusque young stud in a white overall who wanted to roll it on and get the hell out of there, no chippy decorator type snottily suggesting that the smokey taupe shade I was leaning toward looked a wee bit tired, no jumped-up professional who made me feel my life was a failure. (I actually had one of those once, a salesman from a closet redesign company who came into our bedroom, looked at our closet—with my husband's underwear and socks and tee-shirts crammed into a wire basket in the corner—and sniffed: "What you've done to your husband is despicable." Thanks a *lot*.)

Albert had an impeccable wallside manner—friendly, helpful, and without a shred of impatience as I equivocated over Stoneware One and Two, vacillated between the Blue Jade and Empire Green for the kitchen cupboards, and brought in Custard Creme and wiped it off again in the dining room. This went on for weeks.

My son would come home from school, look at yet another swatch of paint on the wall, and say hopefully, "Are you going with this look, Mom?" He even went to a friend's newly painted house and told the mother (who had managed to paint her own house beautifully over a long weekend) that I was "having problems deciding." I guess you could call it a problem that I would break out into a cold sweat whenever a sample went up on the wall and say in a tiny voice, "Oh, so that's what it looks like up."

Albert sanded and basecoated and primed the house, humming happily. All I can say is thank God we negotiated a flat rate. First it was I who delayed the process, then it was Albert, who seemed, some days, to arrive at 10:00 and leave at 10:30. My brother, who never misses a chance to be morally superior, smirked at me over the telephone, "Is Michelangelo finished yet?"

As the seasons changed, Albert was fast becoming Eldin to my Murphy Brown. "How'd that bowling party go for Jonathan?" he would ask. "Did Emily decide on the sleepover?" (How did I end up with a life in which even my housepainter was emotionally present?)

I knew Albert was happily married, but I wondered whether his wife got the same spectacular service that his clients did. You would need, say, new legs on the bed: you would go buy the legs, leave them out pointedly on the bed, and *that very night* you would find them installed. I don't need to tell you this does not happen in a real marriage. Albert was the perfect surrogate husband.

"Albert is amazing," I said to my husband. "Why is he still here?" he said irritably. "I thought he said weeks, not months." "Albert doesn't like to rush things," I said primly. Meanwhile, I kept to myself the news that the friend who had recommended him had recently confessed he was *still* showing up at her house with chocolate croissants and coffee. (So that's where he went at 10:30. . . .)

Our house was a quarter of the size of hers, so inevitably it was finally finished, and, to our minds, perfect. Well, except for the master bedroom, where I had envisaged Tuscany-inspired washed walls, but which came out looking a wee bit *done* (okay, it looked like Caesar's Palace). But Albert and my husband both seemed so happy with it, I decided to get used to it.

Albert stayed away just long enough for us to miss him, and then stopped by to do a touch-up. He oohed and aahed over the kids' new school photos. "That Emily," he said, "what a smile."

Then he broke my heart. "You need some window treatments in here," he said. Thanks a *lot*.

ANOTHER DISPATCH FROM THE MORNING MINEFIELD

*I*t's 8:30 on a school morning—late, late, late—and my daughter has lost her homework book. My son, with unbrushed hair and no shoes on, is sitting at the computer in the kitchen, intently trying to avoid falling into the swamp in an inane game that is emitting an offensive noise. Barely deigning to turn round, he informs me that the lunch I have just packed for him won't do because "that meat is disgusting."

Meanwhile, my husband is buried behind the Shreddies box, unreachable on any known frequency. With my hands gripped around the coffee cup so tightly I'm in danger of snapping it, I contemplate the fact that I have a brutal headache, an impending work deadline, a spectacular sense of my family spinning out of control—and some tuna in the cupboard to redo the lunch.

I don't, however, have a daughter with a homework book. So I shout, in a voice already warmed up by the "disgusting meat" encounter, but now hovering close to Mommie Dearest territory, "WHERE IS THAT BOOK?" and my daughter collapses into tears—something about the harshness of my voice and the burden of all this *remembering* she has to do: if she gets her bed made, she forgets to brush her teeth; if she shows up on time for oatmeal, she goes into a mega daze while she is supposed to be dressing.

As she sobs, something inside of me shatters. I hold her close and tell her that I love her, that I'm sorry I yelled, but that parents get rightfully frustrated when kids don't take responsibility for getting ready on time.

Both children go off to school looking miserable. A few minutes later, I sit at my desk on the third floor of the house, a pile of work untouched. I imagine one of those ghastly film close-ups of an enlarged and angry adult mouth looming: *Where is your hair brush, your homework, your bag?* And the guilt feels like lead weights on my limbs. Of course she should know where her book is, but did our morning have to turn into World War Three?

Since I last wrote about morning chaos, our household finally has achieved an established routine, one that even works. My husband—the oatmeal king—makes the breakfast, our kids not only eat it but manage to do useful things like practising the piano or making the odd bed (very odd). I throw the lunches together, oversee their absolutely erratic grooming (at eight and ten, their hair is always, in their eyes, "fine" unless half a tube of glue is poured over it). I also forcefully urge them to remember their belongings, which normally they are pretty good at doing.

But there are still mornings when shoes are missing, tempers are lost, and spouses are into mutual meltdown, when our family territory becomes a morning minefield, instead of what should be, as the late social historian Christopher Lasch (a man who probably never once had to redo his child's lunch) memorably put it, a "haven in a heartless world."

A teacher once told my husband he could absolutely tell which kids had come to school after a harrowing morning—they were either listless or agitated, but in any case unable to settle into work, unable to learn. Today, the truth is that many kids come to school that way because they are emotionally impoverished, coping with grown-up problems—stress, parental divorce, poverty, despair. But maybe, says a sickening little voice inside of me, they're also coping with an impatient mother who yelled at them.

At noon, I'm sorry to say, I wander over to the school to see if the kids are okay. It's actually no big deal—I'm often around the school anyway. Out in the playground, they are not only fine but puzzled—"What are you doing here, Mom?" And when I try to explain that because of our "bad" morning I wanted to touch base with them ("Was that this morning, Mom?" they ask, genuinely curious), I feel ridiculous.

On my way home, I wonder why the parents I know seem to worry so much about one event, like a bad morning, ruining their children's lives, while losing sight of the bigger picture—providing a continuum of love and support, just being there.

So when the morning from hell prevails, as it will occasionally, I have finally learned to embrace the only thing that works. It is my personal mantra, filled with hope and redemption: in this family, you always get another chance.

"TERRIBLE, HOW ABOUT YOU?"

I arrive at a meeting early, and perfunctorily ask the woman sitting next to me how she is doing. "Black, black, black," she mutters. Within seconds, we slip well beyond the social niceties and head straight for the emotional big time: why are so many women we know depressed or feeling desperately disconnected?

"I don't know what it is," she says, "I just can't seem to feel good about things. I'm tired, I love my husband, but he is driving me crazy, plus I'm trying to figure out how I can do more work, but the kids need me . . ."

Perhaps because I, too, am going through a bad time, characterized by an almost overpowering desire to stand sobbing in the supermarket check-out line, I find our discussion infinitely more interesting than what is on the actual agenda. What I hear is an intelligent, giving woman trying to meet a lot of conflicting needs, and wondering where her sense of joy has gone. But what is fascinating, we both agree, is the historical perspective: weren't many of our mothers depressed like this too? In their day, however, they called it "being blue," and their often vague feelings of unease and disappointment were sloughed off by predominantly male doctors prescribing all those mother's little helper pills.

Somehow, I thought we had reordered the universe, and put the "problem without a name," as pioneer feminist Betty Friedan used to call it, behind us. Women have more choices now, and some of us have more power in our personal and professional lives.

But something remains askew. "I think our mothers may have been angry," my friend at the meeting concludes, "but I don't think they were as filled with self-doubt as we are."

Unfortunately, it's true. Any get-together I'm at rarely includes women brimming with self-confidence: we're too concerned about our children and/or the demands of our work, about the state of our marriage or the search for a relationship, about our parents' or our own health. Some of us are coping with major physical problems that have recently emerged, and all of us are bone tired: "Don't call me after 9 PM" is a familiar cry.

Women in the 35- to 45-year-old age group are also hitting a kind of wall that brings to mind that old Peggy Lee classic "Is That All There Is?"

Well, welcome to real life, those infuriating pragmatists among us would say, and stop whining. They don't want to acknowledge that women and girls are more vulnerable to depression than men and boys, partly because women place a very high premium on intimate attachments. When those attachments are absent, in disrepair, or simply overwhelmed by the stresses of modern life, the emotional cost to women is high indeed. They become isolated, working so hard to meet their basic commitments that there is little time left for social spontaneity, let alone joy and anticipation.

If women are more vulnerable, what are we going to teach our daughters about depression? About the holes that husbands or lovers can't fill, children can't fill, or even work can't fill? What are we going to teach them about what is or is not a fulfilling life? About how to care for their souls, how to balance the emotional budget?

The word that hovers like a mirage in my own life is vitality. Swiss author and psychotherapist Alice Miller has written that vitality—and not the much more elusive happiness—is the opposite of depression. If you are not suppressing your feelings of rage, fear, hurt, and disappointment, whether about the past or the present, you are filled with energy and well-being, open to life.

Some women get there through therapy, others through medication. Many women have surprised me lately by telling me they are in long-term drug therapy, which uneasily brings to mind those pill-popping days of yore. But there are also simpler ways to feel better—using routine exercise to move your body and mind toward a state of grace. Helping others. Friendship—just the sound of a close friend's voice on the phone can lighten the load. Intimate connection—give me a ten-minute walk around the block with my husband (or perhaps yours, just kidding) in which we are really in sync, over a whole day spent trying to connect.

And most importantly, there is telling the truth about our lives. If this had been another era, the woman next to me at the meeting might have said, "Fine, and you?"

And a conversation that lightened the load for both of us would never have taken place.

"GETTING BETTER, HOW ABOUT YOU?"

I am standing at the meat counter in Loblaws, still coping with the unbearable flatness of being, looking at slabs of meat as if I had never seen them before in my life, wondering why domestic life has this power to steam-roll us.

I am not talking here about the joys and sorrows of bringing up children or being part of a family. I am talking about the domestic filler around the heroics—the tasks without closure. Most women I know admit there is always one particular repetitive household chore that sends them into deep, immutable despair. For one friend it is grocery shopping; another told me it was wiping off the place mats after every meal; mine is—oh well, there are several, if you want to know the truth, like putting the groceries away once I get home. But the task that drives me most crazy is emptying the children's lunch boxes every night, cleaning out their half-eaten turkey sandwiches only to fill those plastic containers up again in the morning. As I do so, I can hear behind me the Sisyphean sigh of my husband as he does the supper dishes or empties out our numerous wastebaskets in preparation for garbage pick-up so we can have empty trash cans to fill up again.

I secretly think of solutions to this domestic ennui. The children should of course empty their own lunch boxes, Martin and I could switch chores, or maybe we could wear costumes as we do them—he in a French maid's uniform emptying the garbage, me in *lederhosen* doing the lunches and yodelling . . . the Von Trapped family.

Several hours later, standing at the stove while the singing kettle boils, I burst showily into song, belting out "Amazing Grace" at the top of my lungs—"that saved a wretch like me! . . ." My children are amused, but alarmed. "Mom, are we dysfunctional?" my son asks anxiously. I tell him, "I think maybe 'we' is an overstatement."

The next day, I call my husband at work and tell him I need to break out of my routine. We are not talking an impromptu trip to Vegas, we are talking going to view a house for sale with some friends in the late afternoon, and forgetting, for once, my long-standing obligation to pick up the children from their after-school program. Martin offers not only to pick up the kids but also to have drinks ready if my friends want to come back with me to the house.

In a vain attempt to be helpful, I leave a chicken in the oven with the timer on, but I neglect to notice that the oven is set at 500 degrees . . .

Some hours later, I walk back in, friends in tow. The living room is lit and comfortable, the kids have been picked up, the drinks and hors d'oeuvres are ready, and he does not even mention, until I do, that charred smell permeating the house. "Oh, the chicken was overcooked," he explains benignly. I follow the smoke trail into the kitchen and marvel at his restraint. (If he had burned the chicken, would I have been so understanding?)

"Forgive me," I whisper to the fates, if not to the chicken. "I am happy to be here, in my home, with my little family, on a cold Friday night, whatever angst lurks in my soul." And so it goes, my sense of purpose returning, my spirit growing steadily lighter.

THERE'S NO (WORK)PLACE LIKE HOME

*W*orking at home is trendy these days, partly because so many people don't have a choice any more. As the economy changes, more workers become "self-employed" as opposed to, say, "out of work" (which can mean sitting on the couch crushing beer cans in your bare hands and crying). Instead, engineers and architects, accountants and consultants, management honchos and many others who have become corporate toast, are now swooping down on Future Shops, lugging home enough electronics to start a small telecommunications empire, and then praying for the phone to ring.

I have been working at home as a freelance writer for fifteen years now (minus two separate office-renting experiences when my children were younger). During these years at home, I have been euphoric about my circumstances—and so lonely that my heart sank every morning. I have been thrilled that I could work quietly without interruption—and jealous of everyone who had colleagues, even obnoxious ones, to kibitz with. I have been a writing machine—and pathologically immobilized (friends still refer to a time in my life known as "A Decade Under the Duvet," but surely it couldn't have been quite that long).

I started out on a portable Smith-Corona typewriter, and now have my own telecommunications empire—computer, modem (which I still can't work), fax. My working routine hasn't changed much, except that having school-age children means I must now survive a breakfast hour with the ambience of a Chuck E Cheese outlet before I can regard my home as my office. (And yes, there have been complaints that I lock the door behind my husband and children a little too swiftly when they leave.)

In the silence of a house that is usually over the top with noise— CDs booming, piano practice, shouts of *where's my blue sweatshirt*— I start my working day immensely grateful for solitude. I love being in my house. If I loved it any more, I could probably qualify for membership in the local agoraphobia society. (But then I would have to leave it to go to meetings.)

From a corner of the big window on the third floor, I can watch the wet snow coming down or the trees beginning to bud. The solitude is demanding, but it saves me from one writers' disorder—carelessly flipping my ideas into the conversational pool and watching them swim away. On the other hand, there is no one around to help drown the bad ones. (I recall, in particular, a one-act play I wrote about Margaret Atwood in which her hair was a separate character.)

Working alone can make you eccentric, but there is no truth to the rumour—spread by my neighbours—that I wear pajamas all day long. (There are too daytime clothes made of soft flannel with bunnies on them.) I did once interview a cabinet minister in my bathrobe, but that's because he called back sooner than expected. There is also no truth to the rumour that I spend most of my time lying on the couch, reading old interviews with dead and famous writers, or looking for my horoscope in various magazines. I spend *some* of my time doing this. Occasionally, I will call a friend who has a power job and give her the Leo update on her voice mail, only slightly concerned that her boss will plug into the system and hear me saying, "Get this—'A selfish guy will want you all to himself.' "

On the days when I work well, I have an overwhelming sense of joy. (I never thrived like this in corporate captivity.) And on the days I don't, well, it's still a little voyage of discovery, although what I am discovering may well be Donna Karan, showing her new fall line on *Oprah*. On the days that my kids are sick, I can still get work done, now that they are older. But it's dicey: one minute, I'm at the computer, the next I find myself sitting on the couch with my son watching the bad guy choke on his taco in *Dumb and Dumber*.

I find it a supreme irony that the one virtue I don't even pretend to possess—self-discipline—is almost the only one that matters in the working life I have chosen. Do other people live this dangerously? For inspiration (and to shame myself), there is, on a Post-it note on my wall, a quote from a dead and famous American writer, E.B. White: "A writer who waits for ideal conditions under which to work will die without putting a word on paper." But even E.B. White admitted that, before he wrote, he straightened a lot of pictures.

Before writing this, I took an emotional I.Q. test in a magazine (scoring, according to their results, in the Gandhi range), organized the front closet, rearranged the cushions on the sofa, and then sat on it, drinking my coffee. It occurred to me then that when the home office trend reverses itself—and it will—and many of those architects and engineers, consultants and honchos, are safely back in their corporate offices, I will still be here. Even my horoscope says so.

THE MOTHER OF ALL PROJECTS

*H*ey parents, we have an end-of-term assignment for you! Oh, we know you're fed up with supervising homework, exhausted from debating the merits of the school system, and sick to death of dealing with your child's teacher. But we want you, as a final flourish, to pull together all that you have learned about the ins and outs of school projects this year (preferably in a really neat-coloured Note-Tote available for only $10.95 in your local stationery store). Please answer all questions, and try not to lie.

First, our multiple choice section.

1. When your child comes home and says, "Mom/Dad, I have a really important project to do, and I have to do it perfectly or else," do you: (a) Express delight that your ten-year-old is being given the challenge of writing about an aquatic sea form, in French and English, with four diagrams, a model, and a map to draw? (b) Feel excited by the very prospect of numerous trips to the reference library that will result in you frantically trying to locate material in French on the reproductive lives of penguins, every bit of which your child, now in hysterics, will reject, saying that's not what the teacher wanted? (c) Go immediately to the liquor cabinet for a very

large glass of Scotch? (d) Suspect that the amount of therapy your family needs to survive this project is not available on an out-patient basis?

2. What is the most pertinent question you can ask your child about this project? (a) When is it due, and how can I help you? (b) What in God's name is a diarama? (c) Are you sure your teacher said you had to cross-reference the index? What does she think I—I mean *you*—are, a bloody genius? We didn't even do that in high school! (d) Where do you *think* you left it?

3. What are the strategies you use to get your child to actually do the project? (a) Simply imbue her with the work ethic and then watch her experience the satisfaction of a job well done! (b) Repeat your mantra every hour on the hour— "Have you started your project yet?" (c) Send your child an anonymous note saying if he doesn't finish his project tonight, he will be sorry for the rest of his natural life, and then take away his privileges, one at a time, for every day he procrastinates, ending up with room arrest, a bread and water diet, and no shoes. (d) Call 911.

4. What should your involvement, as a concerned parent, be in the actual work of the project? (a) To offer support and encouragement, supervise a definite work period in which to do it, and occasionally give hands-on help. (b) Once you find out what a diarama is, to spend $20 on material to help your child do a ridiculously overdetailed model of the penguin and its habitat, which leaves you both sobbing because you can't make their beaks look real. (c) Take a leave of absence from your job, and while your child watches or plays Sega, spend the next two weeks putting together a perfectly collated and bound glossy pamphlet, along with a CD-ROM disk, on "The Hidden Life of Penguins." (d) Lie on the couch with the aforementioned glass of Scotch, listening to the Beatles sing "I'm So Tired" from "The White Album,"

and occasionally mutter, in the direction of your child, the Nike slogan: "Just do it!"

Now we come to the essay section! For forty points, discuss one of the following: (1) I like to think my child will be as happy and productive as I was in public school! (My mother still has that A-plus project I did on bears.) (2) I see no irony whatsoever in complaining about the inadequacies of the educational system *and* whining that this project is too damn difficult. (3) If my child doesn't do this project, he will end up making brooms for a living. (4) If I spend any more time with him on this project, I will end up making brooms for a living. (5) Maybe I wasn't cut out to be a parent. (6) Who the hell cares about penguins anyway?

And finally, think of a phrase—not too long!—that sums up your experience with your children's school projects this year. Here are several you can consider: "Richly rewarding"; "Learned a few things myself about aquatic seaforms!"; "Hell on wheels"; "I'm sorry, I'm unable to speak of this without crying"; "I would rather die than do another one."

As for the multiple choice, if you answered (a) to any of our four questions, please do not try to contact me, or in any way share your wisdom, sanity, or superiority with me. I hate you. If you answered (b), relax, you're probably going to be okay. Those, however, who answered (c) or especially (d) should know there is a support group called Parents Against Projects. All inquiries about joining PAP will be kept strictly confidential. (Next meeting, my house. Cash bar.)

WELCOME TO THE TEEN OLYMPICS!

*W*elcome to the Teen Olympics, a soul-stirring spectacle, to be held in a home near yours. (Possibly even yours!) We've gathered together teenagers from around the world, many of whom have been in intensive training, and all of whom are ready to show off their skills in events that celebrate the peaks (or is it valleys) of early adolescent behaviour, behaviour that is designed to drive a parent stark, staring mad, but that is not yet, so far as we know, mentioned in the Criminal Code.

First off, there is Eye-Rolling. To win gold, the teen must not only roll her eyes, but contort her entire face in a way that suggests utter contempt for what is being said to her. At the same site, but in another corner, we have that old subversive classic, Sighing. The louder the better. Following that, there is the combined Eye-Rolling and Sighing, and of course, finalists from that event will be expected to do well in Sulking, which completes, if you will, the Triple Crown of passive aggressive teen behaviour. (The Teen Olympics Committee has yet to recognize Not Hearing as a full-fledged sport in this category, but pressure is mounting to include it, especially from parents who have been Not Heard in extraordinarily original ways.)

For those who like a bit more action, we move on to the Snide

Remark Relay, followed by Lip-Curling and Tongue-Clucking. What you will see here is an impressively co-ordinated team of teenagers, who will notice one little thing about an adult and with the speed of light, will convey this in a round-robin of remarks that are, well, majorly insulting.

The kitchen is the site of our next competition: Opening and Closing the Fridge Door While Looking for Something Good to Eat (Broadly Defined as Anything the Fridge Does Not Currently Contain). The judges will be interested in the sustained length of time the teen can hold the door open, dolefully viewing the fridge's contents while warm air circulates and parents protest, an emphatic slam in which there is a bonus point if that jar of slightly opened dill pickles lands on its side, and a *further* point if the teen indicates she has noticed the overturned jar, but does nothing about it.

Our very popular next event, Asking for Money, can take place anywhere on our Olympic site, although it is usually shown to its best advantage in the master bedroom first thing in the morning, when parents, half-awake or frantic because they slept in, are confronted by a teen's desperate need—new Converse sneakers, say, by three o'clock that afternoon. Cash, cheques, or Visa (the official card of the Teen Olympics) will be accepted.

You've heard about our relays—but don't miss our *De*-lays— Delaying Homework (extra points given for inventive excuses and/or losing text books), Delaying Household Chores, and Delaying Personal Hygiene Moments. Sadly, we have to say that very few teenage girls have proved to be worthy of a gold in the Going a Week Without a Shower event, while males from all countries are showing spectacular times and endurance here. Interestingly enough, though, boys also do well in a mirror-opposite event—The Unconscionably Long Shower, which, if performed properly, can lead to parents sobbing outside the bathroom door while water cascades on and on.

There's something for everyone in these Olympics—the Loud and Repetitive Music Playoffs (Kurt Cobain mandatory), the

Telephone Marathon (extra points for failing to acknowledge incoming calls), the Losers' Triathlon (Misplacing Housekeys, Lunch Money, *and* New Jacket in the shortest possible time), the Self-Absorbathon, and of course, Passing the Buck: "What did you do with my plaid shirt?" is the sort of question most judges expect to hear, and they will be listening for just the right accusatory inflection.

But finally, for most people, the highlight of the Teen Olympics has to be Emotional Gymnastics. When you watch those teens on the Mood Swings, the Unevens, and that old Balance Beam, well, it can literally take your breath away. They'll teeter, they'll fall, they'll regain their toehold, they'll veer from utter misery, through rage and sullenness, and on to a kind of clarity, sweetness, and openness to the world that can dazzle even the most jaded observer. Believe me, there will be very few dry eyes in the house when those plucky kids take their places on the podium for their—and your—final reward. I believe it's called Growing Up.

DIANA'S REVENGE

*Y*oung girls today, or at least the young girls I know, have absolutely no interest in princesses and royalty. Despite fairy tales, despite even the media saturation about a certain Princess of Wales, the concept—or reality—of being a princess registers low on their Richter scale of awareness, let alone ambition. This is a good thing. Imagine if your young daughter took the idea of being a princess seriously, and you had to somehow explain the story of Diana to her. "Well, honey, you see, uh, the Prince married Diana and she became a beautiful Princess, but it turned out there were three of them in that marriage so it was a bit crowded . . ." Oh, forget it.

In the wake of Diana's astonishingly raw confessions on television, I tried to come up with my own satisfactory ending to a princess story that absolutely no one could have made up, simply because it is too, too weird.

First, the bad ending: *After her tell-all interview with the BBC, the Princess was declared "Unfit to Be a Princess" and taken to the Tower of London, where she remained locked up—the Royal Bulimic, the Mad Woman of Versace. (That stunning white Versace cocktail sheath she wore toward the end is on display in the Dianabilia room at the Victoria and Albert Museum.)*

Or possibly: *After her interview, the Princess was shunned every-where, even at the Chelsea Harbour Club, where she still went to work out until, one day, tragically, she exercised herself to death.*

Or even: *After her interview, the Princess, drawing strength from Bette Midler's maxim, "If they can't take a joke, f—k 'em," fled to America, where she appeared regularly on* The David Letterman Show *doing Stupid Princess Tricks.*

As you can see, the possibilities for a very bad ending to this story were endless, which is the main reason, of course, that we all kept watching. But as we watched, mesmerized by Diana's revelations (quickly followed by an order from her mother-in-law the Queen to please, please get a divorce), there was ample reason for even die-hard observers to be fed up with the whole mess: this is embarrassing, can't they do this in private, she went too far this time, the entire Royal Family is filled with, as Jim Carrey would say, *loo-oo-sers!*

But let's go back to the beginning. I confess that, along with mil-lions of others, I avidly followed the courtship of Diana and Charles. I did not totally buy into the fairy tale, but I do remember thrilling to the sounds of the "Trumpet Voluntary" as I watched the Royal Wedding, televised live in the early-morning hours. I remem-ber Diana—was anyone ever that young?—in her golden coach. I remember her walking carefully with her unsteady father up the aisle, stumbling endearingly over Charles's four names during the vows. And I remember afterward, receiving phone calls from other relatively serious women who took time out from running the coun-try to call me and say, "What was with those bangs? They were practically over her eyes!" And, more importantly: "Do you think she'll be happy?"

But there was something amiss. How could there not be when the main qualification to become the wife of the Prince of Wales, other than noble lineage, was simply to be a virgin? Forget compat-ibility, forget sophistication, forget even a sense of duty. What you needed was a negative—no previous sexual history—rather than a positive. And Diana fit that archaic bill.

So a minor aristocrat who otherwise would have lived an obscure existence married to someone equally innocuous, ended up— albeit with her passionate consent—the wife of an aloof older man whose interest in her was, shall we say, nuanced? She gave him domestic legitimacy and those all-important heirs. He was supposed to give her the keys to the kingdom, and some version of happily-ever-after.

And we all know the story from there—*his* mistress, *her* suicide attempts, *his* neglect, *her* lover, *his* ambivalence about being king, *her* desire to hang in there, and of course their children, who have endured their parents' bad behaviour, private and public.

However, with polls showing public opinion clearly on her side, it looks as though Diana's gamble to tell her sordid side of the story paid off. Call it the Revenge of the Sacrificial Virgin. Has there ever been a clearer-cut case of an arrogant institution getting what it so richly deserves? Can we not be a little angry at the sheer cynicism of Charles's courtship of Diana, the chilly grooming of her to become public property, when he had his own romantic agenda, and he and others in the Palace were too dense—or worse, did not even care— to notice that Diana was a pretty shaky candidate for the job?

Any psychology major could have recognized the warning signs: fresh from a difficult childhood (her mother had run off with another man), isolated in boarding schools, intellectually under-nourished. Insecure. Unrealistic. More suitable to be Queen for a Day than Queen of England.

And so she became a valuable asset to her prominent husband at the expense of any emotional fulfillment—she became at once a glamorous star and a neglected wife. She paid a spectacular price. In Canada, we have seen this script before. Does the name Margaret Trudeau ring a bell? And from the look on Audrey Best-Bouchard's face when her husband Lucien announced plans for his own coronation, well, let's hope the Rolling Stones don't tour Quebec City once he's premier. She'll be off like a shot.

Diana is no easily labelled victim, and any attempt to deconstruct her along feminist lines has to acknowledge her uncanny manipulation of the media. It is equally obvious, however, that Diana has endured neglect, public humiliation, breakdowns, and loneliness that would be excruciating if she were a private citizen, but in the glare of the spotlight were enough to drive her crazy. Or make her painfully human, able to connect with ordinary people in a way that no other member of the Royal Family can.

One way or another, we have reached the final pages of this story. The Palace will be scrambling either to knock her down for good or to find a way out of this mess that salvages some dignity— his, hers, and most precariously, that of the monarchy. Which brings us to another ending: *After her interview, the Princess agrees to a royal divorce in which she gets ample money, unlimited access to her sons, and a job as a roving ambassador/princess that she performs shockingly well. Charles carries on as Prince with his lady-friend Camilla discreetly at his side. Years later, after the Queen has enjoyed an unusually long and healthy reign, Prince William finally succeeds his grandmother on the throne. At his coronation, King William delivers a special tribute to Diana (who is wearing a stunning Versace sheath and looks fabulous): "I think we all know how much my mother went through in those early years, and I just want to say how much I admire and love her, and how pleased I am that she and her husband, who adores her, could be with us today. Mum, you're the greatest."*

That's as Happily Ever After as it's going to get. Now if only my daughter were interested in princess stories. . . .

BABES, BITCHES, BIMBOS,
AND OTHER TRUE LIES

*H*aving children alters your perception of popular culture, especially when you begin channel-hopping with them—a popular indoor sport. There they are, waiting to have the world explained to them—ripe for nuance, hungry for image, eager for excitement. And what do they end up with? Something called *Baywatch*.

I discovered the show when an eleven-year-old boy we know reported, mystified, that several boys in his tent at summer camp were bouncing in their camp cots at the mention of Pamela Anderson. Pamela Anderson, or Pamela Anderson Lee, as she is now known, is an eyebrow-raising phenomenon, an actress who may currently be the best-known Canadian in the world. And what is she well known for? I'll give you a hint—they come in A, B, C, and D cup sizes.

If, as Naomi Wolf, author of *The Beauty Myth*, has written, there is such a thing as The Official Breast—large, high, firm, perfectly proportioned, and almost unattainable for most normal women— then Pamela has the ultimate Official Breasts, and they have a starring role on *Baywatch*, a California beach show in which even the sandcastles look structurally enhanced.

With dialogue so banal ("There's been, like, *no* waves, all day") that it makes *Melrose Place* sound like *War and Peace*, *Baywatch* chronicles the lives of a group of lifeguards and seems to be aimed primarily at the teenage market, which means that pre-teens enjoy it.

The show's popularity is not uplifting news. Indeed, it's not even news, but simply Spandex-clad proof that, more than three decades of feminism notwithstanding, nothing much has changed: bimbos, babes, breasts, and—a little further from the show's sunny shores—bitches still hold tremendous sway in popular culture.

I don't mean to do her wrong, but Anderson's character, C.J. Parker, a lifeguard with "a sunny Zen," as her news clips would have it, is not taken seriously even on her own show. The truth is, other blond beach girls make fun of her, accusing their love interests of flirting with her, just because, as someone called Summer snippily put it in one episode, "she was probably running around in something skimpy."

When it comes to portrayals of women in the mass media these days, we are all running around in something a little skimpy. You could call it giving real equality short shrift, despite a surface nod to many tenets of modern feminism. Female news anchors abound, you can see amazingly feisty girl rock and roll musicians on MuchMusic, and in sitcom country, some mighty powerful women ride the range—Candice Bergen's wonderfully mouthy journalist Murphy Brown, Ellen DeGeneres's gently subversive Ellen, and the deeply anarchistic, incomparable Roseanne. (My current favourite line on Roseanne? Her grown daughter Darlene, more snotty and arrogant than usual after being away at school, marches into the kitchen and says to her mother in a contempt-filled voice, "What's wrong with this family?" Roseanne, without missing a beat, replies, "Your father and I are really brothers.")

On the other hand, Marge Simpson, you're wanted in Remedial Feminism 101 . . . and take the Nanny and that Tool Girl from *Home Improvement* with you; but as for that big-haired, brain-dead wife and her equally inane daughter, on *Married with Children*, don't bother. There should be a permanent zap button on the channel changer to rid the screen of them forever.

Such outrage may be bracing, but it is not a simple matter these days to assess how women are faring in popular culture. American author Susan J. Douglas, in her astute and witty book *Where the Girls Are: Growing Up Female with the Mass Media*, puts it this way: "The war that has been raging in the media is not a simplistic war against women but a complex struggle between feminism and anti-feminism that has reflected, re-inforced and exaggerated our culture's ambivalence about women's roles for over thirty-five years."

It's a mouthful, but what it means is, yes, on many prime-time shows today you will see women portrayed as professionals— lawyers, judges, and doctors—but you don't need to be a brain surgeon to figure out that, as women become more powerful in real life, their clothes get tighter and shorter in the make-believe-it's-real world of television.

Baywatch, seemingly innocent of any more complex nuance than "Hey, why put on real clothes if we look this good in bathing suits?," offers up endless variations on the scantily clad theme: women running on the beach half naked, women playing handball half naked, women doing their important paramedical duties, even giving mouth-to-mouth rescusitation, half naked. (Their patients' revival rate is extraordinary.)

Lest that not be enough evidence of babe-ism—i.e. not taking women seriously by focusing primarily on their body parts—the show features most of these underdressed females (haven't they ever heard of cover-ups?) deferring, charmingly, to the male superhero, as played by David Hasselhoff. That would be Mitch, head lifeguard. At least *he* rates a tee-shirt, now and then.

While some of the plot lines, especially those featuring Mitch's adorable son Hoby, are sort of sweet and engaging, the values of *Baywatch*, now beamed world-wide to countries in which the kind of lifestyle the show celebrates might as well take place on Mars, are resolutely conservative: "I guess I don't believe in living together before marriage," muses the much more modestly endowed Stephanie, one of the few non-blondes on the show. Of course, Mitch smiles his approval. (My children nod benevolently from the couch.)

Other television shows are more crafty. They talk a good game, many of the them showing snappy, independent young women going about their lives. But gender equality is simply not, as one of the bright young women on the smash hit sitcom *Friends* demonstrated last season, about ripping open a shower curtain to see a male character's "thing" because he inadvertently saw her "boobies" while she was getting dressed. That's just majorly immature. And besides, didn't we already do this in the eighties with that wacky Suzanne Somers in *Three's Company*?

To get a feel for how kids a little older than my own felt about *Baywatch*, I watched it with my niece, a savvy thirteen-year-old. She enjoyed the slo-mo of actor David Charvet bounding across the beach (himbos get great visual display here too), but mostly she seemed bored. Moreover, she offered a coolly derisive "you've got to be kidding" when asked if she felt she had to live up to the beach bunny image in real life.

However, the teen magazines she and other girls buy today tell a different story. They obsess, of course, about weight—"Ditch flab fast!"—but also about cleavage, about being a babe, albeit in a clever way: "Rule his world in a dress that glows." Some of those prom dresses would not have looked out of place on Oscar night, and one wonders how many a teenage girl feels about having to fill out the top part of the dress.

Pop culture has become increasingly sexualized, and the result may well be, despite the gains made by feminism, a bleak—and dangerous—time for young girls. But the sexualized culture cuts both ways: in a classroom of thirteen-year-old girls I recently sat in on, one said without a tad of embarrassment that she doesn't bother watching the crotches of her male friends "because they're so wimpy."

Which brings us back to those boys in the tent. Are they going to be imprinted like hapless little ducks, jolted into hormonal action only by the likes of Pamela Anderson? Probably not. I also sat in on a lively and poignant, all-boy Grade 8 seminar at a Toronto alternative school, a school that stressed, above all, gender equality. While some boys admitted that the first things they noticed about a girl were "her face," "her breasts," and possibly "her personality," one boy swooned over the Darlene character on *Roseanne*—not your basic bimbo. Moreover, several others seemed truly aghast about the pressure females of all ages feel to look a certain way (not quite conceding, however, their own connection to this pressure).

The search for a perfect body—on *Baywatch*, there is no other—takes its toll on females of all ages, and those young boys had a unique perspective on that: "My mom is always standing in front of the mirror complaining she's fat," said one of them. "I get tired of saying to her, 'Aw Mom, you're not fat, now can I go out to play?'"

Just a little further down the road from the body brigade is the bitch bandwagon. Heather Locklear's venomous Amanda in *Melrose Place* (where, as the show's ads promise, "the affairs are short and the skirts are shorter") may qualify to some critics and many viewers as mindless fun, but there is a nasty aftertaste. People who like women don't build entire television series around such a modern-day Cruella de Vil.

And for real, money-making misogyny, it is hard to top *True Lies*, the Arnold Schwarzenegger/Jamie Lee Curtis adventure spy flick that was one of the top-grossing movies of 1994, a movie that older kids adored, and my kids begged me to rent. From the famous line in the opening sequence in which Arnold (aka Harry) is told to "ditch the bitch" (a cleavage-baring bad girl), it does not go well for women. The bad girl gets smacked hard across the face, called a "stupid, undisciplined bitch," and ends up in a blouse-ripping cat fight with Jamie Lee Curtis. Jamie Lee, playing the smart but ostensibly demure Helen, wife of Harry, is the object of the worst line in the movie. A creep named Simon gloats about her to Harry, not knowing she is his wife: "I got her pantin' like a dog. . . . She's got the most incredible body—a pair of titties that make you want to stand up and beg for buttermilk, an ass like a ten-year-old boy."

It is true that Harry at this point beats up on Simon, but clearly, what he is really ticked off about is that this drooling slimeball is after *his* wife—oh, those property rights. Curiously, the Arab Defamation League complained about the movie's treatment of Arabs, who are the story's main villains, but there was nary a peep from any quarter about its treatment of women. Is this, too, just mindless fun, and if so, what message does it send to male viewers of all ages?

As for female viewers, we can take heart from author Douglas's opinion that among all these persistent television and movie images of babes, bitches, and bimbos, women were, and are, capable of "finding feminist empowerment in the most unlikely places." From watching Joan Collins on *Dynasty*, for instance, says Douglas, you could learn how to be assertive in your own life.

Perhaps this could mean taking away from *Baywatch* the resolution to be a stronger swimmer. But if you're really interested in sexual equality, you might be better off drawing your own line in the sand. *Click*. In our house, we didn't even have to arbitrarily turn off *Baywatch*—our kids blew it off themselves a few weeks after first watching it. For them, Pamela Anderson was nothing more than a tempest in a D-cup.

THE TERROR LOTTERY

*W*e tell ourselves stories in order to live, wrote American author Joan Didion. Women are good at this—we dish, we share, we keep each other laughing and give each other hope with our revelations about our marriages, our kids, our jobs. One of the darker threads that knits us together, unfortunately, is fear—of being stalked, attacked, murdered. Most women have a story like mine, maybe not as dramatic but certainly, to them, as painful. These are the stories we'd rather not tell, but occasionally, they surface—especially if there is a run of similar stories in the news. Then we remember. . . .

It was fifteen years ago, and I had recently moved, alone, into a charming first-floor apartment in a renovated house. My bedroom window faced onto a back alley, and while there were curtains in the bedroom, there were none in the dining room, making me visible from the street.

Late one night, the doorbell rang. I was not alone in the house—Martin (we were not married then) had come in, and was in the bathroom. I walked toward the door, listened, heard nothing, and started back down the hallway. Suddenly, coming toward me, was a man with a black stocking mask over his face. I remember thinking, "Where did he come from?" before I was engulfed by sheer, blind terror. I screamed, and screamed for Martin to hear me over the noise of running water in the bathroom. I also kept moving, dancing, almost like a boxer, as the man in the mask tried to get hold of me.

Martin heard my screams, and holding the only weapon he could find—a curtain rod—he raced, yelling, at the man, who escaped out into the street. The police arrived quickly: the woman below me in the basement flat had called them. There was something in their matter-of-factness that terrified me further. They told me that the man had probably lurked in the alley, and thus had missed Martin's arrival. The man had rung the doorbell to get me out of the bedroom, so he could slip in through the unlocked bedroom window. "If your boyfriend hadn't been here. . . ." The policeman let the sentence trail, as I sat shaking on the sofa.

In different ways, the experience shattered both of us. It was good for me to know that something so innately dark as a masked intruder had brought out the fear in a man, too. Martin had saved both of us, but he too had seen how helpless you could be in the face of what had been, for us, an incredibly violent few minutes. What if the guy had had a knife, a gun? What if he was still out there, stalking me?

I was living elsewhere when the police reached me two weeks later. The man had returned, through the window of the basement suite of the young woman who had called the police on my behalf. This time, he also carried a long nylon scarf. And this time he got caught. An alert neighbour had called police.

He was charged in the second incident, but not in mine—I couldn't identify him anyway—the police told me. That was fine with me. Desperate for normalcy, I didn't even call to find out what happened to the case.

I did call the rape crisis centre one day when I realized that fear—amorphous, incapacitating fear—had settled inside me and would not go away. I couldn't even walk alone to the bathroom at night. You did the right thing, the counsellor told me. You screamed, you moved around—your instincts worked for you. She gave me back a modicum of the enormous amount of power and independence I had lost.

We read about countless victim impact statements in the media, and the litany becomes banal: *it changed my life forever. Now I am always afraid. I will never trust men again.*

Well, I didn't stay afraid forever and I never lost my faith in some men. Since the Paul Bernardo trial, and its revelations about young women being stalked and murdered, I have thought a lot about what happened to us, and about how to keep our children safe— now and later. In some ways it is easier now, because they are still subject to supervision, street-proofing, and our own eleventh commandment—on certain urban streets thou shalt not walk alone. But how about when they are adults? I could get cynical here. The masked intruder—hah, that's the long shot. What about spousal battery? An ex-lover going after you with a hatchet? How does one deal with the myriad dark possibilities and not rob one's children of the sense of joyous connection between men and women?

First, there's urban safety: don't rent a street-level apartment. Put up curtains. (I'll pay.) Lock your windows. Moreover, I hope that both our son and daughter will recognize the signs of obsessive love—a love that could kill them—jealousy, physical aggression, psychological coercion. I hope they emerge from their childhood with healthy egos, strong bodies, and self-confidence.

None of which, I suppose, except for curtains and a locked window, could have prevented what happened to me. In the terror lottery, I got one of the worst-case scenarios—the masked intruder—and the best possible outcome, total rescue. I guess I was one of the lucky ones.

GIRLFRIENDS

$\mathcal{E}$mily and her friend Kiva had a sleepover the other night at Kiva's house, and then (hadn't they had enough of each other already?) asked if they could play together all the next day. Back at our house, they were heavily into a complicated game involving horses, a secret identity, and what appeared to be ropes tied around their legs. I say "what appeared to be" because every time I entered the room, these two eight-year-old girls, each of them possessed of more *sang-froid* than I, as an adult, can muster on a really good day, would pause delicately, smile sweetly, and say, "Could we please have our privacy?" In other words, butt out.

I shut the door after offering them a snack and went downstairs, thinking back to my own girlhood, my own best girlhood friend, Vicky, and that glorious, intense, even subversive connection that two girls who are close friends can have.

Our friendship grew in the most natural way—we lived across the street from each other, and from the age of eight on, we were soulmates. I was skinny and mouthy and full of secret fears and grandiose ideas. Vicky, tall for her age, with a striking headful of curls, was quiet and a bit passive. "Those feelings of being trapped inside myself," she said to me recently, "They were worse after you moved away."

We walked to school together every day, two little girls gradually growing up until, at age twelve, we had attained what we thought was the height of sophistication. Slaves to fashion, we would go shopping downtown on Saturdays, dressed the same in red and white gingham shirts, white pleated skirts, dark nylons and white running shoes that we cleaned up with white polish. Both blondes, we put lemon jello in our hair to make it blonder, and then laughed hysterically when we left the gelatin on my hair too long and it turned into straw. Our bible was *Seventeen* magazine, and we calculatingly eyed every fashion model, every new look. That green houndstooth checked jumper, could we pull it off? We were there to tell each other we could, to bat back the doubts that began to engulf us— about our faces, our bodies, our beings—as we entered adolescence.

Vicky was the only person I could really admit the truth to—I didn't measure up. In another house, further up the street, Helen Bahinski once made mincemeat out of me when, standing in front of her full-length bedroom mirror, she bragged, "My sister says I have the perfect face and figure for a twelve-year-old." I cringed inwardly in the corner—without a sister or a body to brag about. My body failed me in ridiculous ways—I was obsessed about my too-thin legs, and may well have been the only girl in school to have padded ankles—I wrapped Kleenex carefully around my ankles underneath my knee socks to make them look fuller. The advent of Twiggy saved my life. Suddenly, the most famous model in the world had toothpick legs, just like me.

As soon as I could race to Vicky's house from Helen's, we ridiculed the perfect twelve-year-olds of the world and plotted our revenge. We spent hours talking, just talking—in my bedroom, on the front lawn, in her living-room, on our way to school. We taught each other to dance in her parents' living-room listening to a Lou Christie record, "Let's Dance." We would stand at opposite corners of the room, and then pony to the centre, our faces solemn. Dancing was a serious business. It meant the start of dating, romance, it meant some guy might actually like you. Together, we spied on Vicky's glamorous older sister. Desperate for sexual clues, we once caught her necking—or was that petting?—on the couch with a James Dean clone who struck us as the quintessence of danger and charm. She shocked us by getting pregnant, and subsequently married at seventeen. It was on our usual Saturday shopping spree that Vicky broke the news to me, and we stood crying together in the Simpson's shoe department.

We shared every adolescent milestone, from getting our periods (mine came well after hers), through our first bras, and on to my first kiss—a disaster that took place in the Williamson Road school yard when a boy I liked shoved me against the wall and went at me—the tongue, the tongue, nobody had warned me about the tongue.

The last summer Vicky and I were together, before I moved, we shared our greatest adventure: we had already fallen in love with the Beatles. We both loved George, I think because he wasn't quite at the centre of things, because he seemed, to our naive and ever hopeful souls, *gettable*. What was it about this group that brought an entire generation of young girls to its knees? They were sexy but safe, and never before had we been given (or given ourselves) the permission to, well, scream out our desires, to sob with love. (You certainly couldn't do that with a boy your own age.)

Just before we were to enter Grade 9, fearful of high school, boyfriend-less and gawky, Vicky and I decided to run away to spend the night with the Beatles. They had arrived in town for a concert (we had tickets) and a stay at a downtown hotel. I left a message for my parents, scrawled in red lipstick on our bathroom mirror, saying I was sorry, but we just had to do it. Packing our cheese sandwiches and furtively setting off, we felt we were finally on the edge of a breakthrough, that our real lives were about to begin.

We planned to sleep on the street outside their hotel, along with thousands of other screaming girls, all of whom were in the same sexually agitated state.

A few hours later, our parents unceremoniously braved the crowds to retrieve us—how could they spot us in that seething mass

so fast?—and we were forced to beat a humiliating retreat.
Nevertheless, we sat smirking in the back of the car as we were driven home. It was still the most daring thing we had ever done, and we had changed because of it. We felt badder, and braver—brave enough, even, to start high school.

The world that Vicky and I created for each other was warm and forgiving, and while we fussed at each other—she found me bossy, I found her implacable—it protected us for a long while from that other world of girlhood cruelty and taunts, of competition and failure. Of betrayal. But when I was fourteen, our world changed drastically. That summer, after crying till my eyes were puffy and telling my parents I just wouldn't go, I moved away from our downtown neighbourhood, away from Vicky's house, away from our high school, and into a new suburban neighbourhood and a strange, huge, new high school. I was terrified.

Early in the fall, still lonely for those old familiar faces, I returned for an all-important after-school dance at the local Y. Vicky told me on the phone that a boy named John was interested in her, and the dance was crucial—it just might be the big moment they would get together. On the bus, on the way to the dance, I was nervous. I wore a new denim pea jacket, and an air of complete desperation. I was overwhelmed by insecurity—I no longer belonged there, I certainly didn't belong yet at my new school, and I was also jealous that Vicky had a boy interested in her while I did not.

Once I got there, I turned into a maniac. To the strains of "Woolly Bully," I began aggressively, madly, flirting with the boy Vicky liked, until he literally had no choice but to dance with me. I walked away with him, and left her standing there, shocked and angry and more hurt by me than she had ever been in all our years of friendship. I danced every dance with him. Vicky left, devastated, and shortly after the dance was over, I left, alone too, with a horrible let-down feeling in the pit of my stomach, to take the bus back to my new neighbourhood. I never saw that boy again.

I like to think the feeling in my stomach as I left the dance was the beginnings of shame. It would take me a few more years, however, to learn the lesson of loyalty to one's own sex. I got burned, too, along the way, sometimes unknowingly. Only recently, an old high school friend called to reminisce, and in the middle of our conversation, she told me she had run away to New York one weekend with Dean, my Grade 12 boyfriend. My boyfriend? New York? "Oh," she said, "don't you remember, you two had a fight, and he asked me to go away with him and I did." Even thirty years later, I was incensed. *How could she?*

Vicky and I made up—we were never able to stay angry with each other for long. I apologized then, and today, I'm still apologizing. Now, when we get together for lunch, or with our husbands and children, we joke about the betrayal: *"How could you?"* she'll say. We heard later that the boy turned into a wife-batterer, so maybe I did her a favour. But I still can't listen to "Woolly Bully" without guilt. Luckily, it doesn't come on the radio too much any more.

Vicky and I have been through a lot together over the past thirty years—our dating days, the death of her first husband (eight months after their marriage, of an aneurysm), my marriage, her remarriage, the births of our children, the challenge of working, of being mothers, of growing into middle age—and still wondering how to make our hair blonder. (She still has that beautiful headful of curls.)

There are friends today to whom I am closer, to whom I talk much more frequently, drawn together by what we do for a living, or who we've become, or by the compelling history we've shared since then. But no one will ever replace Vicky for me. Vicky knows my eight-year-old soul. . .

After a full day's play in their own little world, Emily has just said goodbye to Kiva at the door (they will be on the phone with each other before bedtime). Tired, she snuggles up with me on the couch. "Mommy, will I be friends with Kiva when I'm grown up?" she asks. I answer, "I don't know," I answer truthfully. And then I ask her, would she like to hear that old Beatles album again?

SAVAGES

*C*all it practice love: at a certain age, girls create a brutal emotional world of intense friendship, conflict, betrayal, and in some lucky cases loyalty, as they learn through these friendships, literally, how to have relationships with the rest of the world.

I stood in a Grade 6 classroom not too long ago and watched two girls—top dogs in their little world—strip the gears off another girl who was clearly, in their eyes, and maybe in her own, a loser. "This is the disgusting Sarah," one of the cool girls said to me, while Sarah, clearly not as cool, in appearance or demeanour, hung her head pitifully. It was a moment of emotional brutality, and I wished so much that Sarah would fight back but she didn't. You never do, at that age.

One woman I know recently told me that that early-adolescent cruelty marked a turning point in her life. The day she showed up in the school cafeteria to eat with her three best friends as she had done for the past four years, and they simply told her they didn't want to be with her any more, dumping her without any explanation, was her first major heartbreak—and the beginning of a loss of confidence in all her relationships.

That early adolescence is still, for girls, a time of "unparalleled nastiness"—as one child psychologist has put it, is a thought that makes many women of my generation feel uneasy, as if we haven't done our job. Weren't we going to promote sisterhood from the cradle on? To our dismay, there is also a heightened physical brutality between girls today, a proliferation of girl bullies. There are more and more incidents of girls cutting each other up with knives, kicking each other, beating each other up to the point of hospitalization, as well as being pathologically mean to each other.

Those are extremes, but I see my daughter, still young, already heading out onto the jagged rocks. In her circle of eight- and nine-year-old girls someone is always "breaking up" with someone else. (The words are almost identical to those used of male/female relationships, and the relationships themselves are as complicated and passionate as a Russian novel.) Words like "bitch" and "hate" get used, tantrums are thrown daily, and some girls' lives are made into a living hell.

An educator hot on the trail of gender equality once told me he thought the escalating numbers of girl bullies could be traced, despite the gains of feminism, to the continued dominance of the patriarchy. At a certain age girls begin to sniff the awful truth— they will only have a limited amount of power to play with, and so they reach out and grab whatever they can, squashing their friends in the process.

Yet even taking into account the negative side of girl friendships, I think that female friendships are in better shape now than they used to be. Women are teaching their daughters (and themselves) that it is a shell game to betray other women for the attentions of men. Mothers are more alert to the pitfalls of girl friendships today, ready to intervene (sometimes to the annoyance of their daughters) to say, you can't treat someone like this, or you can't be treated like this. "Just once I'd like her to take my side instead of telling me the other girl is just insecure," one eleven-year-old girl in the thick of girl-to-girl combat moaned to me about her mother.

Women today are also showing their daughters by example what good, strong, durable female friendships look like. When any number

of my friends call, both my kids have no doubt as to their importance in my life. (Occasionally, I have let the dinner come to a bad
end on the stove as I listen to a friend.) Sometimes they are my life-
line, and sometimes I am theirs.

Teachers today play relationship counsellor (a role that was
almost unheard of for a teacher in my school days) and urge girls to
view themselves and one another differently, to cut each other
some slack. I watched two teachers run a girls' softball team last
spring and I was amazed—and touched—by the level of support the
girls, encouraged by the teachers, gave one another. A girl, with terror in her eyes, would completely flub her time at bat, and invari-
ably, one of her teammates would yell, "Nice try, Sophie," almost to
the point where it became a joke. Once, the principal wandered by
and laughed: "If this had been the boys' team," he said, "one guy
would have already said, 'He sucks, do we have to have him on the
team?' "

To find out more about girls' inhumanity to girls, I recently had
a conversation with an eleven-year-old who spent a year of her
school life being unpopular. She agreed to tell me what it was like,
so long as I didn't use real names. I'll call her Jennifer.

Smart, perceptive, a fanatical reader, and a crack swimmer,
Jennifer has a forthright manner, remarkable eyes, and a sturdy
body. Last year, she found herself isolated by a group of girls in her
neighbourhood, some of whom she had known since early childhood. "I'm not a follower," she says, groping for an easy explanation
as to why, when she went out her front door every morning, expect-
ing to join this group of girls walking to school, they would stop
talking, then quickly walk on ahead of her. When, another day, she
asked if she could play with them, they said no, giggling as they
walked away. "Don't ask," counselled her mother, slightly frantic for
her daughter. "You have every right to be with those kids."

But there was one girl—Brittany—who ruled the roost, and had
since kindergarten. What Brittany said was the law. Tight shorts
were out, boxers were in. And Jennifer was definitely out. Just like

that. Brittany, whose authoritative (and authoritarian) fashion tips came to her courtesy of a cooler older sister, was able to turn an entire group of girls against Jennifer, whose insights into her tormentor are both telling and sad: "She has a bad life," says Jennifer, explaining that Brittany's parents are divorced and often fight over her, and that Britt, who in the earlier grades had looked like an emerging leader, now merely packed a lot of anger.

Jennifer is from an affluent family in a comfortable neighbourhood, and her parents—progressive, concerned, involved—have done all they can to support her. But watching her ordeal has been excruciating. Her mother cracked once, berating one of the girls on the sidewalk for excluding her daughter, and then wished she had kept her mouth shut. Her father preferred to talk strategy with her: "Have you tried this?" he would ask, coming up with yet another retort.

Jennifer was dogged. She would try to impress the group by saying something funny or sarcastic. But the girls would go silent, all of them staring back at her, until one of them said haughtily, in sitcom-perfect sarcasm, "What's your point?"

She had other friends, but somehow she couldn't walk away from these snobby girls, she couldn't let it go. Once, she accidentally fell off her chair in class, and when she saw how they laughed, she tried to do it again and again. Recalling this now, she is embarrassed: *what I did for love.*

The tide eventually turned for Jennifer—as arbitrarily as she was ostracized, the group now began to accept her. Brittany's boyfriend apparently thought she was funny and liked talking to her. (Ironic, of course, that a boy's opinion swayed a group of girls.) So she is now, precariously, on the fringes of popularity. It is still scary, though, for her to look back and remember how alone she felt, scarier still to know it could happen again. Recently, in Jennifer's new semi-popular phase, the other girls dared her during recess to kiss a guy. She didn't want to do it, but she was frightened that if she didn't, all the bad treatment would start up again, so she took her time walking over to him and was literally saved by the bell.

Then there was the matter of school dances, which had just started up for her Grade 5 class. She went to one and liked it a lot—she wore a body stocking, overalls, and her mother's long earrings, and she asked guys to dance and was asked to dance in return. The next dance, however, got trickier, when she found out that Brittany and a few others were plotting way ahead of time who was going to dance with whom. She talked it over with her mother, and she decided, instead of letting her anxiety get the better of her, to opt out of the dance, with the excuse, which was partly true, that she had a family party that night.

Jennifer thinks back on the grim year she spent, and says if she had any advice to give to other girls going through it, it would be: "Don't beg for forgiveness, or for people to like you." She believes the worst is over, but her mother is not so sure. "I hope it won't be hard for her if the going gets tough again," she says carefully, in front of Jennifer. After all, she hasn't hit junior high yet, and in junior high, as American author Jane Hamilton succinctly put it, "the girls are like savages."

BUILDING A BETTER BOY

*H*e can ride a bike like the wind, expertly cruise the Internet, and almost bake a lemon poppyseed cake by himself. He knows, on one hand, how to ask caring questions—"How was your day, Mom?"—and on the other, how to engage me in nuclear-level verbal warfare. He can read a room emotionally, but he still can't figure out why his own temper blows sky high. He knows the names of the Three Tenors but has never played a complete game of hockey in his life. Jim Carrey, with his swaggering walk and rubber face, is one of his comedy heroes, and noise—loud, CD-playing, in-your-face noise—is his middle name. He is ten years old, and he's the most wonderful—and maddening—son in the world.

Bringing up a boy these days is tricky. It smashes some of your preconceptions about gender, reinforces others, and makes you think, if not worry, constantly—is he going to turn out all right? Most of the conversations I have with mothers of sons today have more than an element of high anxiety in them.

Feminism has changed the boundaries of what is considered normal behaviour for boys, as they push themselves—or allow themselves to be pulled—over to what used to be, according to the rigidly defined gender roles of the past, the girls' side of social behaviour. There are, of course, many boys for whom weapons are still the only acceptable accessory, but then there are others like my nephew, an eleven-year-old who skateboards fanatically, drums in a band, wears an earring, and along with his two best friends, enrolled in a baking class last summer. His shortbread was wicked.

Some people claim that society today is robbing boys of their gender inheritance—the right to make fart noises, throw spitballs, and push each other face down in the school yard. They worry that we are turning them, instead, into distaff females, docile and controllable even if it takes a dose of Ritalin to do so. More boys than girls are prescribed Ritalin these days after being diagnosed as having Attention Deficit Disorder, a condition in which the child can't settle into an activity, has trouble focusing, or is hyperactive. While I don't agree that boys are being neutered—you can see too much evidence to the contrary on a visit to a school yard—there is indeed a remarkable Ritalin culture out there. The kids call it "taking hyper pills."

Women who have thought at all about sexual equality—and about the shortcomings of the men we love—are intrigued by the challenge of bringing up sons today (or building a better man, as some of us in the cabal secretly refer to it). I've taken several overt steps—I've talked to my son about sexism, and I've encouraged him to be more emotionally aware, not only of his own feelings, but of other people's. I've urged him to take responsibility for the emotional lives of others.

Slowly, though, we are letting go the notion that boys, and men, are emotionally illiterate—largely, I think, because we see they can change. There will, however, always be boys and men for whom "feelings" are the yuckiest thing around, and even for sensitive boys, too patent a focus on feelings can make them justifiably want to arm-wrestle someone.

Socially, life is cruel for boys in very different ways than it is for girls, although the bottom line is still about whether you measure up. Lots of boys still get called wimps for the same old reasons— they're not good at sports, they're sensitive, they admit to an interest in something considered girlish. Lots of boys are still locked in the straitjacket of machismo. But many others now move more fluidly across gender lines, partly because of the efforts of their mothers, but also because their fathers, in a low-key way, are showing their sons their own softer sides.

The fathers I know register the same concerns about their sons, but I don't think they agonize in the same way mothers do. I wistfully see my son and my husband, for instance, casually going off to bond over a bike ride and a swim, while I'm left behind, limp as a dishrag on the couch after a scorching emotional conversation about the disaster that was his day. It's as if, for now, the bike-riding closeness is enough with his dad, but somehow the intimacy that he and I have ended up with is verbal, and much more intense. And yet everything I have read and heard about a boy's adolescence tells me that this will change—that he will, in effect, clam up—so I better get my bike ready as well if I'm going to stay close to him.

The way we treat boys today is loaded with contradiction, which points up our own ambivalence about changing sexual roles. We tell our sons that it is okay—even desirable—to cry, but then, when they keep crying into junior high, we get nervous. Is he tough enough? And when it comes to sexism, boys are being taught and taught and taught again what they cannot say to and about girls, but they can also legitimately claim that so far, it doesn't work both ways—girls can walk into a room, torture them psychologically or even physically (I've seen it happen), and if they take the bait and go berserk, hey, they're sexist toast, down in the principal's office, having to discuss their *feelings*. "When I say something bad to a girl, it's sexist," says one teenage boy, "but when she does something to me, it's retribution."

Not too long ago I went to an alternative school at which the teachers firmly believed they actually *were* building better boys. I sat in on a seminar of thirteen-year-old boys and they were, well, adorable. Slightly nerdy, much less sophisticated than their female counterparts, they nonetheless had a wry grasp of sexual politics. The topic for that day was "Are the girls here more assertive than at other schools?" and the answer was perhaps most poignantly expressed by one boy who, when asked about his ideal girl, responded, "Someone who is nice and won't beat me up."

These boys easily admitted they stared at a girl's breasts (but felt slightly guilty about it). "I've, like, looked at a girl's body without caring and knowing about the rest of her." But they also seemed horrified by the pressure girls put on themselves and each other to look good. "Why do they *do* that?" asked one boy. "They're always going, 'Oh God, look at my hair!' for no apparent reason." But the boys worried, too, about not making the sexual grade, about not being the "hot hunks" the girls talked about constantly.

They also laughed at themselves for not being as verbal as the girls: "When we have a mixed class," said one boy, "if you look at the speakers' list, it'll be girls girls girls talking about some show on puberty, while a guy mutters about computers in the background."

What was interesting was that the teacher leading the seminar—a feminist who was, it turns out, profoundly worried about her own teenage daughter's self-confidence—had previously led an all-girls seminar during which she seemed earnest and concerned; but with the boys, she relaxed and laughed, telling one of them at one point to "put a sock in it." It was as if she could enjoy these boys, especially their foibles, without identifying too closely with them. We both laughed out loud when one boy confessed sheepishly, "I say to myself I must take a shower tonight and then something cool comes on TV and I don't take a shower for a week."

I came away from that seminar reassured about some of the boys of today. I only wish I had been able to bring that lightness and sense of hope to a dinner party I had attended some time before that class, at which every woman at the table confessed she was worried about her pre-teen son—he wasn't living up to his academic potential, he had fallen in love with the nastiest side of heavy metal rock, he was hanging with guys who weren't good for him, he was lonely and sad, and insecure, he was aggressive and obnoxious, he was, well, he was a handful.

To reassure one friend with a younger boy, I offered to lend her a book I had read and liked, *The Difficult Child*—only to find it missing from my bookshelf—already loaned out to another desperate mom with a son who was, if not difficult, then "different." We seem to have trouble distinguishing between the two.

We all live with the fear that we have the square-peg kid, and sometimes we assume too readily it's our son's problem, when it could easily be a bad fit with the school, the teacher, or his friends. My heart did a little flutter downward the day my son, a year or so ago, after having been given the video of The Three Tenors performance, asked me hopefully which of his friends did I think might want to watch it with him. How about none? But why was it necessary to care what his friends thought?

Instead, I should have popped the popcorn, watched it with him, and quietly celebrated what a special kid I've got: he is able to carry on an articulate conversation with just about anyone, he's great (most of the time) to his younger sister, and enormously competent—our trip navigator, our official memory, my aide-de-camp for Loblaws expeditions (although if he rams the cart down the aisle one more time making that stupid motor noise I'll. . .).

What kind of man will he be? I can't wait to find out.

EMILY WILL BE THIRTEEN IN THE YEAR 2000

I once interviewed a self-styled femme fatale who stunned me when, flicking a scarlet fingernail, she said she wished so much she could have a daughter so "all this knowledge won't be wasted." Was it perfume tips we were talking here? I don't think so. In any event, I, who did not have children at the time, wish I could be that certain, now that I do have a daughter, just what it is I want her to know, and what I can teach her about being female that will actually come in handy in a world of sexual complexity and gender conflict.

Emily will be thirteen in the year 2000. As she goes about the very serious (it seems to both of us) business of growing up, she takes my breath away with her emerging determination, her sense of self, her courage, her humour . . . and yes, her beauty. But, of course, every parent unabashedly feels that kind of visual adoration of their children—you literally cannot take your eyes off them. Already I can see her developing artistically. She draws, she writes, she creates stories out of her life. I often wonder what story she will tell of her own girlhood, what she will later say was missing or unfair. It won't be a close relationship with her father, opportunities for playing baseball, or, having bubble baths—we've got those covered. (It just might, however, be a horse—some girlish passions are timeless.)

Emily is operating in a world that is, at least on the surface, very

different from the one in which I grew up. I remember most of all
the admonitions: sit with your legs together . . . don't swear . . . be
nice. . . . And later on, the sense of not being at full throttle. I was
always pulling back, biting my tongue, thinking no one—no boy,
anyway—will like me if I say this or do that.

At first glance, the girls of today seem transformed, even physically—they look at home carrying a battered catcher's mitt, wearing
tattered sweats but sporting gorgeous filigree earrings and hair dyed
aubergine. And on the surface, they seem to be far more outspoken and
assertive than I ever was. They have learned the lexicon of liberation:
they are encouraged to study female heroes, they are quick to mouth
the ideals of equality. "Joel is so sexist," a seven-year-old girl will
mutter of her classmate. "He thinks girls can't play hockey."

The girls of today do play hockey, talk dirty, and thanks to the
saturation of mass media values, are enormously, if selectively,
sophisticated. But still their actions belie their words: I watched a
school baseball coach chastise her girls when, during spring training, they would muff the play and then meekly say sorry. "Never say
sorry," shouted Louise, the teacher. She was fierce about it—there
was no need for them to apologize. Boys never would—they would
just learn from their mistakes and move on. I have also discovered
that, between the ages of, say, eight and eleven, girls—and not
boys—seem to preface every mildly critical remark they make with
the words "No offence, but . . ." I finally had to point out to my
daughter that she didn't have to say "No offence" when she was
telling me she didn't like a certain television show, that she had a
right to her opinion and there was no need to apologize for it.

There are more chilling contradictions: these same "assertive"
girls, when in their early teens, call each other sluts if they happen to be popular with more than one boy, and yet are at enormous risk for AIDS because they still aren't bold enough to tell a
guy no glove, no love, no matter what the slick department of
health advertising slogans say. They are girls who will smoke
themselves blue in the face, seduced into thinking that nicotine

gives them style and strength rather than a shortened life span.

What is going on here? In *Reviving Ophelia*, a provocative book published by Ballantine/Random House, American psychologist Mary Pipher paints a grim picture of lost girls, who are at risk for eating disorders, depression, drug abuse, and plunging self-esteem. That landscape of lost girls has been previously painted—by American educator Carol Gilligan, whose books (*In a Different Voice, Meeting at the Crossroads*) have become the basis for all modern feminist theory about young girls. Gilligan maintains that early adolescence is a time of heightened psychological risk for girls—they tend to lose their voices, and their spunk. In her chilling estimation, girls come to realize, mainly through subtle societal pressure, that in order to have relationships, they have to give up some essential part of themselves. In short, they lose their authenticity. If this is true, then my daughter is heading toward the peak of her powers now, and by the year 2000, she will be . . . subdued.

But Gilligan's approach has come under recent attack, most vociferously by Christina Hoff Summers, another American academic, who claims in *her* highly provocative book *Who Stole Feminism?* (published by Simon and Shuster) that Gilligan's self-esteem analysis was flawed, that girls and boys suffer equally as they navigate adolescence, and that in fact, girls are the stronger.

I stand somewhere between these two polarities, believing that some of the same old discrimination against girls continues unabated in the schools today, and that they are indeed living in a culture that wildly contradicts itself when it comes to what is expected, desired, or available for females. But I also believe that we are on the brink of inventing a wholly modern girl.

I can see it in my daughter. We're veering toward creating complete human beings here with no awareness at all that certain avenues are closed to them, at least because of their sex. In researching the lives of young girls, I came across the work of Elaine Batcher, this time a Canadian academic (and to my mind, the most perceptive of the lot), who studied the mall culture of young girls in the eighties. In an article that appeared in *Atlantis: Women's Studies Journal* (published by the Institute for the Study of Women, Mount St. Vincent University, Halifax), Batcher wrote that one of the real gains for girls in our time is "freedom of association and the resulting normalization of friendship between the sexes." It's true. Girls and boys today have much more casual, less intense relationships. They date, if you can call it that, in groups, and in some ways it seems a lot healthier than being paired off at fourteen.

Batcher wrote about what she called a woman's sphere: "Never, not even today, has the circle (a woman's sphere) been congruent with the sphere of human existence; it has always occupied part of the whole." Think of the current obsession with Jane Austen and the female heroines she created, and how eclipsed their lives were, how completely dependent they were upon a man coming forth to marry them, how shattering it was if that man did not show up, backed out, or turned out to be a cad.

Today, young girls (and their mothers) can see that circle widening all the time, creating possibilities that are shimmering out there on the horizon. But how, *how* are we going to get there? I contacted Batcher, an independent education consultant who now writes fiction in Toronto, to find out if she still believed in what she had written in the eighties—that the current obsession with self-esteem is a healthy step on the road to real accomplishment, and that out of all this agonizing, really new women will be created: "Women who know the past, understand their debt to the past, but do not feel the need to re-create it. They will be women—not girls-for-life, and not surrogate boys."

"Well," she said over the telephone, "I was hopeful, wasn't I?" Her views have been tempered by having raised a daughter, who is now seventeen and heading into what Batcher sees as the Generation X wasteland. (When she wrote her earlier statements, her daughter was around the same age as mine is today, which may have accounted for her optimism.) "If you look at women's history," says Batcher carefully, "you'll see that every hundred or so years, we believe we're inventing a new woman. But she keeps getting cut off at the knees." Batcher cites as evidence the current backlash against much of the feminist thought of the last decade or so. And, like Pipher, she laments the sexually dangerous climate for girls today in which they are pressured to enter the high-stakes world of sexuality at an earlier and earlier age, unprotected (ironically, in the name of progress and liberation) by the very restrictive rules that in fact sheltered them in the past.

I wondered, after I spoke with her, whether I was being a Pollyanna in thinking our daughters were headed for a brave new world, one perhaps even more integrated than the one we live in. They are growing up with mothers who work, in families that are coping as best they can in the face of the tremendous time pressures and ecomonic stresses of the nineties. Most of us, ironically, have earned the right to work at two exhausting jobs—out in the professional world by day, and then tackling our domestic chores. Many of us have partners who help, but I don't know a woman who can claim a 50–50 split with her mate when it comes to housework and childcare. Our daughters are well aware of our fatigue, but they admire us in a way we never did our own mothers. In her most recent book, *The Hite Report On the Family: Growing Up Under Patriarchy*, Shere Hite, the sociological surveyor a lot of people love to hate, maintains that more young women like and respect their mothers now, than her surveys showed in the seventies— young women then were disgusted with their mothers' marital subjugation and passivity. But that pendulum, too, can swing.

I'm sure these same young women are privately weighing the bargains we have made, the anger and frustration we exhibit about how the domestic burdens still fall mainly on our shoulders. These girls are no doubt saying: "I can do better than this." I hope they are saying this.

On a personal level, I need to admit my own conflicted impulses. I want to protect her forever, but I want to be better at letting her live large. I want to not be embarrassed by any inequality in my marriage, but I also want to tell her and show her, yes, it is possible to have a thriving partnership with a man and not lose yourself in the process. In terms of self-image, I try never to trash my own body in front of my daughter (sometimes the lip-biting is severe), not because I don't want her ever to think I have doubts about how I look in leggings, but because society gives girls enough ammunition with which to trash themselves without their mothers leading the charge. One of the unsettling experiences of having a daugther is seeing a perfectly formed little girl (and her friends) eyeing themselves critically in the mirror, coming up with judgments someone must have taught them: too fat, too thin, ugly, thick nose, bad hair. She will, I hope, never think I am obsessed with either of us being thin, and if there is an element of hypocrisy here, well, that's what humour is for. All I know is, the only member of our family who will ever be placed on a diet is our cat—and he is a boy.

Today, although she is bombarded by relentless media images and messages that exhort her to stay thin, get sexy, and dumb down, my daughter can also see, through the prism of popular culture, all kinds of women achieving all sorts of different things. Sometimes we forget that thirty years ago, *this simply was not the case*. I was struck, watching the movie *Apollo 13*, by the actual news footage of the era, and how incredibly *male* it all was. Today, even in the O.J. Simpson trial, a long-running saga that was admittedly about one of the most dispiriting issues facing women and men today—domestic violence—there was the ubiquitous image of Marcia Clark, day after day, competently prosecuting Simpson.

My daughter does not even know yet about the countries where they mutilate or kill or refuse to educate the girl children, or, in this country, about the stalkers, the rapists, the wife-batterers. Or the people—men and women—who truly believe that because you are a woman, you are not entitled to the whole sphere. And I do not know if we are raising our girls to be the women they need to be in this complex world. I suspect we won't know for a while.

In the meantime, I will try as best I can to assuage her doubts about herself and her abilities, to point out all those contradictions to her. Have the courage to be yourself, I will say. Tell the truth about your life. Aim for love and respect. Live large. Grab it all. I will wish her joy—and then, I promise, even if I have to bite my lip again, I will let her find her own way.

GAY PRIDE AND
MOCKINGBIRDS

*I*n our family, we don't consciously set out to deal with the big
issues of the day. They come up, often unexpectedly, in the
course of a conversation, a school experience, a day in the life. Or,
on a sunny Sunday, smack in the middle of a long weekend, when
we all have no particular place to go. . . .

This Sunday is an early summer beauty, warm and bright, but it's
tinged with moroseness, primarily because no one has invited us
anywhere. In lieu of sitting around our backyard whining, or worse,
being forced to shoot baskets for pennies with the kids for the rest
of the day, we quickly go the high-concept route: "Let's have an
Urban Day!" I announce brightly. The kids look justifiably suspi-
cious, but soften soon enough when I suggest (a) rollerblading at a
downtown patch of circular concrete set up to accommodate in-
line skating—with a ghetto blaster blaring to keep them hopping,
and (b) a stroll over to Yonge Street to catch part of the Gay Pride
Day parade. That word—parade—always gets them. Yes! (I have a
slight ulterior motive—either I've always been out of town for the
parade, or I've just never been able to go, and I'm curious—is it a
wild party as well as a political statement, do the people on the
sidewalks get caught up in it, will we see any great sequinned cocktail outfits?) Martin is fine with both activities so long as neither

involves whining, at least on the part of immediate family members.

How do you prep your children for Gay Pride Day? At eight and ten, they have so far asked only basic questions about homosexuality. What do gay men or women do together anyway? They have also cautiously felt their way around their—and our—attitudes toward homosexuality. We have close friends who they know are gay, friends who, because of their humour, warmth, and the interest they take in the children, are high up on their list of desirable guests. Our friends live much like us, only better—a larger, more elegant house, more disposable income, which often leads to jokes among us all: now this, *this* is a lifestyle.

At the rollerblade rink, Martin and the kids skate for an hour while I stroll over to check out the sidewalk situation. The corner is already jammed, and I find myself surrounded by parade participants. A party-hearty bare-chested dude with a paper cup of beer in his hand enthusiastically offers to hoist the kids up on his shoulder after I tell him I'm waiting for them to arrive. I laugh and say thanks. I start fidgeting, though—the kids aren't here yet and they're about to miss Dykes on Bikes. (How do you tell the kids that lesbian women can refer to themselves as dykes but hey, we better not?) The Dykes on Bikes are kind of disappointing anyway, the only good sight (in my estimation) being one woman's magnificent iridescent purple evening gloves, which go way up past her elbows as she sits on the back of a Harley.

Finally, I see the kids and Martin worming their way through the crowd. A woman in a wheelchair, along with her companion, call out to me that they have made some room up front for the children to sit down, so off they go. (Everyone is so welcoming and polite, it's beginning to feel like . . . Miss Manners goes to the Gay Pride Parade . . .) In the meantime Martin, in baseball cap and bermuda shorts, is hanging back, a little shy, until the bare-chested man with the beer cup beckons him forward after hearing me call him Mar. "Mar!" he echoes, "come on through!" Martin laughs and moves up front to be nearer to me. The man chats happily with us about our

children, what grades they are in, what they're learning. He tells us
that he is the vice-principal at a senior elementary public school in
the suburbs, and "no, I'm not going to tell you which one," he says
pointedly. His discretion is understandable, since he's veering
between being naughty and nice. A kilted bagpiper goes by and The
Vice (as I've now come to fondly think of him) yells out, "I can
blow, but I'm not too sure about the piping!"

The parade unfolds at an excruciatingly slow pace—lots of placards, lots of waiting, and finally, here come the drag queens. A
Diana Ross look-alike sashays by, preening and pouffing, followed
by a dead ringer for Dame Edna. "Get a leg wax!" yells The Vice.
Craning my neck to see them, I study the kids' faces—they seem so
impassive, I wonder whether they even know that it is men they are
watching, and not women. Later, they tell me they weren't sure.

I ponder the drag queens for a moment. Unlike other drag shows
I've seen, there doesn't seem to be much sexual energy here. Far
more vital are the hordes of young men, some of them pinup-poster
gorgeous, outfitted in kilts, or shorts, and tight tee-shirts. They look
a bit serious, very dashing, and yes, happy, and it's not hard to feel
happy for them. In previous generations, young men have killed
themselves—and probably still do—rather than admit to such longing and lust. These boys and men seem to be sexy and touching and
brave. And alive. I wonder why it is, even on Gay Pride Day, that
the gay men seem so much more flamboyant and visible than the
gay women.

The kids, meanwhile, don't look very happy. Later, they tell us
they were put off by the male bystanders yelling come-ons at the
drag queens going by. It offended their propriety, as did the sight of
two bare-chested men kissing: "It was so gross." One could put it all
down to the rampant homophobia that still thrives in their school
yard, except kids at that age don't particularly like to see anyone in
any gender combination kissing, especially with their shirts off. A
"gay families" contingent marches by with a few children waving
shyly. (Do those kids *like* this? I know my kids would never march

in a "hetero pride" parade and wave to the crowds—they would be mortified.) Along, too, come the inevitable and important signs angrily urging a cure for AIDS now.

The mood feels communal and warm, but very adult as well. Looking around, I see that apart from our kids, there are no other children spectators at this corner, and furthermore, there are not all that many straights simply standing there, applauding. Many of the spectators appear to be gay as well, lining the streets as an appreciative audience, or perhaps just sticking a tiny toe out of the closet.

At the climax of the parade, a red convertible cruises by carrying two elderly men dressed in pink shirts, holding bouquets. Like stately homecoming queens, they are at once sending up the moment and enjoying it. They represent the old guard—the "queers" that our parents' generation were familiar with—quiet, effeminate men living lives that didn't bother anyone. Our parents could accept this, could feel safe and superior at the same time to this cautious coupling, rather than these flamboyant, deeply exhibitionist young men and women of today flaunting their prowess— and their choice—as they take over a downtown street.

The two older men in the convertible are from British Columbia, and are famous for having fought a legal battle to have their relationship recognized so that one could receive the other's pension benefits. They lost the battle but won the war, making the news everywhere with their elegant argument for equality.

"Those guys are great," says Martin, and I wonder whether they feel safe to him, too, a world away, at least on the surface, from the boys in kilts, and universes away from, just coming up now, the S&M crowd. One guy, leathered up like a Nazi, with a pinched mouth and a waxed moustache, strides by cracking a whip, while another man holds up a sign that says: "Hurt the One You Love."

My heart does a freefall. I think, what are we doing here, what mistake in judgment is this? I look at Martin, and he seems sombre, too, for the first time. "You guys are going to have some explaining to do," says The Vice, but I'm not sure we are, or at least not the kind he thinks. The kids, about three feet from us at the edge of the side-walk, have turned around scowling, as if to say, *enough*. But they're not passing moral judgment on leather chaps as daytime wear. They are bored out of their skulls. *You call this a parade?* Emily actually mouths the word "Bor-ring" in my direction. Not enough jugglers. Of course it's hard for her to understand this parade is not simply about entertainment, it's about being brave and defiant, it's about taking a stand, about celebrating the right to do so. But it's also about making your sexuality the central issue, instead of just a part of the whole. It's still about *us* and *them*.

As we walk away, The Vice gives us high marks for "exposing your kids to this." Basking in my liberal tolerance, I don't tell him that I'm seriously wondering if it was the right thing to do. Jonathan and Emily are not cracking smiles, and as we walk back toward a little café on a side street, they are both grumpy and puni-tive. Over brownies and iced tea, we tell them a bit about the two men in pink shirts, and they ask a few desultory questions before they get on to something that really fires them up: could they have a yoghurt smoothie?

In the car on the way home, I wonder if we should say something further about fear and prejudice and homophobia. Young boys just edging their way into puberty and coming to terms with their own sexuality are terrified that they might be gay. Young boys and their mothers, it seems. Many mothers breathe audible sighs of relief when their pubescent boys—despite their single earrings and dyed hair—start showing an interest in girls. "Thank God, he's straight," women say to each other, because the other would be so, well, dif-ficult. The other might entail a parade.

Back home, after some burgers on the grill, we decide to rent a movie, and Emily suggests *To Kill a Mockingbird*; she caught a glimpse of it one night on television and thought the little girl in it—Scout—looked like a friend of hers. My eyes widen in Martin's direction. Another big issue? Can't we just rent *Ace Ventura, Pet Detective* and call it a wrap?

But the movie—in black and white—turns out to be so riveting that we let the phone ring on and on while we watch. Based on Harper Lee's wonderful novel, the Oscar-winning film, made in the sixties, is about a disturbing rape trial in the American south in the thirties. It is about racism, about children coming of age, about innocence and experience, about people being different from one another, but most of all it is about character, and how you find yourself in situations that show you either have character or you don't.

Martin and I sit there, me with the occasional tear in my eye, explaining the adult parts to the kids. I start to worry about the message in the movie that the woman—poor white trash if ever there was any—falsely cried rape. Enough! I think to myself. If I can't deal with any more social complexity tonight, then certainly our children cannot. Better just to focus on the story and on one tiny message: that, just as it's a sin to kill a mockingbird—to kill something that did nothing but make people's lives happier with sweet music—it's a sin to expose, exclude, ridicule, or hurt other people just because they are different.

The credits roll, the kids go reluctantly to bed. They are scared out of their wits by one scene that takes place on Hallowe'en night, when Scout and her older brother are attacked by a madman in the park. What will their dreams be like tonight, I wonder—hairy-legged Diana Rosses in cocktail regalia dancing with overall-clad black farmers? Lynch mobs with pitchforks chasing marchers waving gay rights placards?

Martin and I take tea and leftover brownies from the café to bed. "I just love those times when you're teaching your kids something," says Martin. But I wonder just what it is we taught them. Nothing, it seems, except maybe old movies, is in black and white any more. It's all shaded, filled with complications, contradictions, and ambivalence. Or does raising a family make it so?

Martin sighs with such an aching sadness and sweetness mixed up together that I wonder whether we are thinking the same thing: we're honouring a moment that won't last, cannot last. We had a whole day of saying to our kids: look at this, let me tell you about that, come with us, you'll find this interesting. Already we have friends and relatives whose children have "turned" on them, on that great voyage through puberty, and into adolescence, the voyage where, if they're doing their jobs, the children have to leave their parents behind.

I go to sleep thinking of how we began the day—aimless and grumpy, and how we ended it, together, after what seemed like a long journey. My idea of family expands and contracts like this every day. When we are all out of sync it feels onerous, wrong-headed, a terrible idea. But when it works, it's like a waterfall of good feelings, so fresh, so light, so pure.

I wish our own mockingbirds sweet dreams—and strength of character. Before morning comes, they both will be camped out, blissfully asleep, on our bedroom floor.

LOVE AND MARRIAGE

*I*t is the month of love, and the dark of winter. Approaching Valentine's Day (that great Hallmark consuming opportunity), I find myself meditating on my marriage when I'm interrupted by the ringing telephone. It is yet another woman friend calling to say, "How can I offload this jerk?" I wonder, am I the complaints department of modern life? Or maybe a secular domestic priest(ess) whose confessional box is the telephone.

Those complaints hover in the air, reminding me of their truth: "*He promised me he would organize our daughter's birthday party—did he not see me angrily stuffing twelve loot bags while he channel-surfed in the living room?*" "*I worked all day, made dinner, cleaned up, and then he has the nerve to comment on my lack of a sex drive!*" "*He comes in at night, saying he wants to spend time with us, gives the kids and me an absent-minded hug, and then sits down to read a report. . . .*"

Ah, modern marriage. That continual search, against all odds, for connection, for intimacy, for a moment the soul can revel in. When it is bad, it is so very bad. You long for a connection, you think you are the only one without it. You imagine, everywhere, happy women whose partners are standing in the kitchen looking a little like Hugh Grant (well, maybe not Hugh Grant, that bastard) but anyway looking tousled and handsome, drinking a glass of wine and wittily recounting their day as you recount your own.

Instead, whimpers one woman, "I just want a husband who comes in and doesn't fan the mail before he acknowledges me." Instead, moans one man, "She is always *at* me. No matter what I do, it is never enough."

I take cover from all this domestic disharmony in the words of Joseph Campbell. Campbell is the late American mythology professor who, during a series of interviews he gave in the 1980s to Bill Moyers on PBS television (later collected in a book, *The Power of Myth*, published by Doubleday), rivetingly discussed the nature of love and marriage.

Modern marriage as a concept, says Campbell, began in the twelfth century with the troubadors, who went in search of the perfect love, describing it as "perfect kindness." Before the troubadors, love had simply been identified with Eros, the god who excites you to sexual desire, a biological urge. Then, love was transformed into the highest spiritual existence, and the courage to love—to choose one's life partner—became the courage to affirm one's own experience against tradition.

In a committed marriage, says Campbell, love "is the high point of life," and the only point: "If marriage is not the prime concern, you're not married." Campbell does call marriage "an ordeal—the submission of the individual to something superior to itself," which is exactly how I see it on a morning when I am having trouble even with the sound of my partner chewing his cornflakes. But Campbell's words urge all of us on to higher ground: "The real life of a marriage or of a true love affair," he says, "is in the relationship . . . here I am, and here she is and here we are. Now when I have to make a sacrifice, I'm not sacrificing to her, I'm sacrificing to the relationship."

No friend I've ever talked to imagined her marriage would be as hard as it really is. To my mind, the terror of thinking you're with the wrong man is surpassed only by the terror of thinking you're with the right man—and it's still this difficult. But Campbell manages to transform marriage into a romantic, even a heroic struggle. What he celebrates is the sharing of pain—and destiny—with another human being. Most love affairs, says Campbell, last only as long as they benefit both parties. But a marriage? "A marriage is a commitment to that which you are."

Why do these words seem so thrilling to me? Lately, I confess, I have been regarding my own husband with renewed astonishment. His good qualities, were they there last week? His smile, for instance. His grace and equanimity on family excursions when I have lost it and feel like lying down on the ground. His day-to-day resilience, his ability to master on the piano, after much practice, a Chopin waltz, which, when he finally gets it right, fills the house with its lovely sound and and makes me forget those hours of relentless practice that produced it. His tremendous civility. His arms around me at night.

Isn't perfect kindness that morning cup of coffee he brings me after I stay up most of the night agonizing over a child's problem? Of course, if we were in a down phase, I would point out he chose to snore while I worried.

But I have just finished reading words that seem, to me, more powerful—and certainly more sexy—than any trumped up message on a card could ever be. Sexier still because he gave them to me to read. *Here I am, here he is, and here we are.*